Xo Dad & Paula,

Merry Christmas 1990
Happy Coffee Table Reading!

Love
Annie + Mickey

The Nova Scotia four-masted schooner *Ada Tower* came ashore at Sayville, Long Island, New York, on May 23, 1923. The Bay of Fundy vessels were built to take good ground with no damage. The sandy shores of Long Island did not harm the hull. The *Tower* was later pulled off the beach and went back to sea. *Photo courtesy of Paul C. Morris, Nantucket Massachusetts.*

SHIPWRECKS
ALONG THE
ATLANTIC COAST

By William P. Quinn

A chronology of maritime accidents
and disasters from Maine to Florida.

The British Brig *Matilda Buck,* from Gonaives for Boston with a cargo of logwood, went ashore on January 9, 1890 about a half mile from the Wood End Lighthouse in Provincetown at the tip of Cape Cod, Massachusetts. The crew was rescued by wreckers throwing a line on board and sending off a boat. *Photo courtesy of Cape Cod Photos, Orleans, Massachusetts.*

Black smoke billowed from a fire which completely engulfed the 2,300 ton Panamanian freighter *Beth* in the Caribbean Sea, 90 miles south, southwest of Santo Domingo, Dominican Republic. The burning vessel was photographed from a U.S. Coast Guard plane in March, 1964. The vessel was enroute to Martinique from Port Arthur, Texas, with a cargo of lubricating oils and chemicals. A lifeboat from the Liberian freighter *World Jonquil* pulled alongside the burning vessel and rescued twenty crew men. Later, they were transferred to the Coast Guard Cutter *Aurora* and landed at San Juan, Puerto Rico. *Photo courtesy of the U.S. Coast Guard, Washington, D.C.*

Library of Congress Catalog Card No. 87-63412
ISBN-0-940160-40-4

Printed in the United States of America by:

Arcata Graphics-Halliday, Braintree, Massachusetts.

Published by:

Parnassus Imprints, P.O.Box 335, Orleans, Massachusetts 02653

FIRST EDITION

Other books by
William P. Quinn

SHIPWRECKS AROUND CAPE COD (1973)
SHIPWRECKS AROUND NEW ENGLAND (1978)
SHIPWRECKS AROUND MAINE (1983)

PREFACE

A shipwreck is a spectacular event. The Atlantic coastline between the Canadian Maritimes and the Gulf of Mexico is strewn with thousands of wrecks. Coastal shipping in this area is active the year round and has been since the mid seventeenth century. The wrecked hulls lie interred in the shifting sands between the inshore waters and the continental shelf and beyond to the deepest part of the ocean. This book is primarily a collection of photographs beginning in the late 19th century. Some of the 100 year old pictures are spotted while others may be a little faded. Many are sharp and clear which shows the careful attention to detail made by photographers of yesterday.

An old cliche suggests that: "one picture is worth ten thousand words". It is possible to write an entire chapter describing only one photograph of a shipwreck. To appreciate the old photos, one has to realize the hardships the early cameramen had to cope with while making some of their pictures. They traveled mostly on horseback or in a buggy with the big glass plate cameras. This is in contrast with a modern, hand-held, thirty-five millimeter camera. A photographer today could shoot a whole roll of film while his counterpart of yesterday was setting up to do just one picture.

Pictures of maritime accidents appeared almost coincidentally with the development of the photographic art in the late nineteenth century. The areas covered in this book include primarily the United States coastline from Maine to Florida. The information presented is the result of extensive research in maritime museums, old newspapers, historical society records, personal interviews and contemporary reports. It would be impossible to list all of the wrecks that have occurred, about many of which there is no knowledge. The official reports tell of scores of ships that sailed and "went missing", filling the tragic pages of history with mysticism. The reports of pirates, ghosts and mermaids are numerous and sometimes entertaining. But the true stories are often stranger than the legends.

Today, modern technology has reduced the number of shipwrecks somewhat, but not entirely. The majority of maritime accidents are still caused by the adverse weather. The evidence of storms sinking large ships was graphically displayed in 1983 when the 605 foot long bulk carrier *Marine Electric* was lost off the Virginia coast during an ocean gale. It was Herman Melville who said: "When beholding the beauty of the ocean skin, one forgets the tiger heart that pants beneath it". The shipwrecks will continue as long as man sails on the world's oceans.

This book is dedicated
with love to my granddaughter:
Eva Michelle Quinn

Off the coast of Cape Hatteras, North Carolina, the four masted schooner *G.A. Kohler* was battling a hurricane on August 23, 1933 when she was cast ashore. Her crew of eight men and one woman passenger were rescued by a Coast Guard lifeboat. Later the hull washed up on the beach and lay there for years. She was burned for her scrap metal just before World War II. *Photo from the collection of Fred Fearing, Elizabeth City, N.C.*

CONTENTS

1   Atlantic Coast maritime history. The early voyages, trades routes along the coastline. The Massachusetts Humane Society. The Mooncussers and the Life Savers. 1

2   The Revenue Cutter service. The Atlantic derelicts and their paths. The sailors superstitions and illusions. The Portland Gale of 1898. 17

3   The diverse Atlantic Coastline from Maine to Florida. The development of the wireless radio, Jack Binns, the hero of the *Republic*. 35

4   The decline of the sailing ships. The loss of the *Titanic*. The North Atlantic ice patrols. The establishment of the U.S. Coast Guard, World War I. The Atlantic is conquered by the airplane. 49

5   The beautiful lighthouses along the Atlantic coast. The era of the rum runners. The S-4 tragedy and the loss of the *Vestris*. 69

6   The saga of the Lightships. The *Morro Castle* disaster, the hurricane and aftermath in 1938. 97

7   The outbreak of World War II. The fire aboard the *Normandie*, the submarine warfare in the Atlantic and the loss of the *Oakey L. Alexander*. 115

8   The grounding of the Battleship *Missouri*. Two tankers break in half off Cape Cod. The aircraft carrier *Wasp* collides with the destroyer *Hobson*. 143

9   The birth of the electronic age. The *Constellation* fire and the loss of the Atomic Submarine *Thresher*. The Coast Guard battles drug smugglers. 170

10   The Chesapeake Bay Bridge-Tunnel closed by a ship collision. The modern Lloyds underwriters. Environmental concerns about oil spills and the wreck of the *Argo Merchant*. Dangerous pesticide cargoes. 180

11   Underwater wrecks. Amateur divers seek treasures. Looking into submarines on the bottom. The Brig *de Braak*, the *Santa Margarita* and the Pirate ship *Whidah*. The discovery of the *Titanic* wreckage in 1985. 195

12   The loss of the *Marine Electric*. Modern ice patrols. Loran navigation. The Maritime heritage of the United States. 217

The line drawings in this book are by Paul C. Morris of Nantucket, Massachusetts. Mr. Morris is a noted marine painter who is also a scrimshaw artist and maritime historian.

Above: The *City of Worcester* hit Cormorant Reef off New London, Connecticut on May 28, 1898. The vessel came into the harbor where she sank. Her passengers were removed and the vessel was pumped out. She was refloated six days later. **Below:** The Schooner *Daylight,* with a cargo of 1,000 tons of coal sank shortly before noon on January 18, 1910, in Lower Bay, New York after she struck a partially sunken mud dumper scow. The Captain and crew were saved and the schooner was refloated on March 28th. *Photos from the collection of Paul C. Morris, Nantucket, Massachusetts.*

CHAPTER ONE

The maritime history of America began along the Atlantic coastline. It opened in the fifteenth century and the stories of shipwrecks along this seaboard vary from tales of anxiety and drama to many of panic and terror. Often they tell of bravery, sometimes cowardice, rarely humor. The accounts of the disasters fill volumes and depict legends. The romance of the sea is portrayed while the reports of tragedies explore the frailties of man. Along the coast, grotesque evidence of groundings and shoreline wrecks protrude like anonymous tombstones out of the beach sands. The ocean floor, reaching out to the edge of the continental shelf is littered with the decaying skeletons of thousands of unfortunate vessels that were victims of storm and fog, collisions and fires. Several have been noted in the world's headlines when famous people were lost. More were listed in the local newspapers as unique happenings while the majority were enrolled in the maritime journals as statistics. The thousands of vessels that sank at sea, have their bones scattered along the ocean floor. Some are deep, and, until recently, were beyond today's salvage technology. Others lay in the shallow waters of the continental shelf and are periodically visited by modern salvors who dive into the intrigue of sunken treasure.

One only has to mention the name *Titanic* to conjure up memories of the greatest shipwreck in modern history but there were many more. Some with higher loss of life, some equally poignant and a few more, equally tragic. The earliest recorded shipwreck was chronicled about 2,000 years ago. The Bible relates that St. Paul was cast ashore on the island of Malta and the vessel became a total wreck, ACTS-Chapter 27. The Atlantic coast has had many tragic disasters. Along this seaboard countless thousands of vessels have piled up on the rocks and reefs with disasters recorded on every shore. Christopher Columbus sailed west from Europe in 1492, and his flagship, *Santa Maria* was wrecked in Caracol Bay in what is now Haiti.

The U.S. Atlantic coastline is approximately 1,500 miles in length but the actual measure is much greater because of the numerous rivers and bays. An example is the state of Maine whose coast measures 288 miles from Eastport to Kittery. But with a myriad of harbors, inlets, islands, and coves the actual length of the jagged, rocky coast is 3,478 miles. The earliest Atlantic coast exploration is believed to have been carried out by the Norsemen about 1000 A.D. Not all historians agree as the evidence is not conclusive, but it is difficult to prove or disprove. Other European discovery voyages to the western Atlantic region began in the late 15th century. One of the early explorers, Verrazano, warned others of the shoals, shifting sand bars, shallows and the lack of useful landmarks for navigation. A large majority of the 16th century wrecks occurred along the reef lined Florida straits and Bahama banks when the Spanish treasure ships sought a short cut to the Atlantic. There is evidence of a large number of these wrecks and modern day salvors have, in the past few years, reaped fortunes from the ocean bottom off the coast of Florida.

Settlements began to blossom along the entire coastline and maritime trade flourished between the colonies. Trade routes were established from Canada, down to the West Indies. The growth rate of cities and towns along the coast was rapid. Baltimore, Philadelphia and New York became leading maritime centers of population. When the colonies banded together and fought the war for independence, the expanded trade routes had caused a marked increase in maritime commerce. However, there were no significant improvements in marine safety and shipwrecks increased in alarming proportions. Navigational charts improved safety somewhat but the sailing ship was at the mercy of wind and weather. Disasters continued to plague the mariner and losses were mounting with regularity.

The Civil War (Federal) transport *Oriental* came ashore on May 8, 1862 on Bodie Island, North Carolina, just south of Oregon Inlet. The vessel was never pulled off and part of her boiler and stack are still visible just off shore today. *Aerial Photo by the Author.*

Often, travel by a sailing vessel along the Atlantic coast was hazardous. Experienced navigators were rare and the few aids consisted of a magnetic compass, a leadline for sounding, some crude charts and a few lighthouses equipped with weak whaleoil lamps. Unfortunately, many of the experienced men were lost in shipwrecks and this delayed progress in safety. The 19th century was to go in the record books as the worst period of wrecks along this coast. The reasons were many and varied. Most were weather related, caused by the storms that frequently swept up the coast. Ships were sunk far out at sea with very few survivors. Fog blinded the mariner as he returned to port. This resulted in many ships, cast high and dry up on the beach. There were several other causes of wrecks: capsizing, fire, collision, icebergs and arson were but a few while human errors resulted in numerous accidents. Sometimes, sailing vessels were undermanned when crewmen became ill, got drunk or were exhausted and could not carry out their duties. Other losses occurred during wartime when ships were torpedoed or hit mines. There were some extraordinary disasters recorded in the early days. A New York Maritime Register report on October 30, 1872 stated: "Washington, Oct. 23 - The U.S. Consul at Liverpool has furnished to the Department of State an affidavit of a seaman, who was on board the steamer *John Straker* (of South Shields), Purvis, Master, which arrived at Liverpool Sept. 25 from Boston. The steamer sailed from Boston, September 5, and the seaman stated that: On the same night, when 35 miles out, they ran down an American schooner, but the steamer kept on her course without stopping the engines or trying to render the schooner any assistance whatever." During the fall and winter months, many vessels sailed and were never heard from again. Even with today's electronic communications and space-age navigation, this type of event still occurs.

In the late 18th century, the Massachusetts Humane Society was established to relieve the sufferings of the sailor cast ashore. Small closed sheds were erected along the beaches with canned foods, firewood and first aid kits. The odds were none too good for the mariner as he first had to survive the wreck, make his way across miles of beach and find the Humane Society shed, then hope that vandals had not eaten all of the food or used up the wood. The only other aid for the shipwrecked sailor was the wrecker on his daily trek down the beach. In 1871, the U.S. Congress improved the Life Saving Service. The stations, crewed by local men with a background of life near the sea, were built along the Atlantic and Pacific shorelines as well as the Great Lakes. When the Government Life-savers began to answer the distress signals, the fatalities along the coast decreased. The storms and the wrecks continued but many lives were saved that would have otherwise been lost. The veterans began to spin yarns and mystical legends were created about the mariners' adventures, related often during the long winter nights around the home fires.

The wreckers capitalized on the ever growing toll of disasters along the Atlantic shoreline. These men made their living by roaming the coast, looking for wrecked ships to save what they could. Some were saints but more were sinners. They were called pirates, thieves, poachers and scoundrels. They were sometimes life-savers, occasionally rascals and often plunderers but they were usually the first to arrive at a wreck scene and many persons owed their lives to these Privateers of the beach. The general rule was that, the first one to arrive at the wreck had his choice of salvage. This did not always hold true as weather conditions played a part in the operations and heavy seas could cost the wrecker his life if he were not vigilant. When more than one wrecker was on the scene, the competition for the spoils sometimes erupted into violence. Shady practices were not uncommon among the wreckers. Ships were sometimes lured ashore with false lights. This practice was alleged to have occurred along the entire coastline. There were unconfirmed reports of strange wrecks at Monomoy Island off Cape Cod while further to the west, ships were said to have been lured ashore at night by unusual lights, displayed by some outlaws on Long Island. In New Jersey the Barnegat Pirates were reported to have stolen a few cargoes while further south at Cape Hatteras there is a town named "Nags Head" after the legendary practice of tying a lantern around the neck of a horse and leading him over the dunes. These nefarious deeds were reported as far south as Florida but the stories have been handed down through the years and no doubt embellished each time

Above: On the stormy night of December 26, 1872, the Hamburg barque *Frances* was wrecked on the beach at Truro, Massachusetts, one mile from the Highland Lighthouse. The vessel was badly iced up with a northeast gale blowing at the time of the wreck. Cape Cod Life Savers rescued the crew of 14 by surf boat. *Photo courtesy of Mystic Seaport, Mystic Conn.*
Below: The remains of the Hamburg barque *Frances* lie in the surf wash and are visible from shore at low tide in the Highland area. The remains of iron hull have lasted over 100 years. *Aerial photo by the Author.*

they were told. To the wrecker, the primary concern was the profit realized from the disaster which was probably welcomed in the local economies. The wrecking profession flourished into the mid-19th century until the Federal Government began to erect more lighthouses and install additional aids for navigation to ameliorate the carnage on the Atlantic coastline.

The Government did not take any action along the shoreline until hundreds of vessels had been wrecked and thousands of persons had lost their lives. In the annual report of the operations of the U.S. Life Saving Service for the year ending 1876, one of the articles detailed the early apathy toward protecting navigation:

"The dangerous character of our seaboards suggests the nature and the urgency of the means requisite to their comparatively safe navigation. These might reasonably be expected to early occupy the attention of a maritime nation, a great extent of whose boundary line, from the beginning of its earliest history, presented a formidable array of dangers, and to excite the concern of its merchants and the benevolent instincts and sympathies of the humane.

"It appears, however, that the Government was exceedingly tardy in discharging even the paramount duty of lighting the salient points of the coast and of ascertaining and appropriately marking its dangerous localities. In 1820, it maintained but fifty-five light-houses. It had surveyed no portion of the coast; and for a long period we were chiefly dependent upon foreign nations for the charts and sailing-directions used in the navigation of our waters. These were very inaccurate and unreliable, and were superseded by the better work of the Messrs. Blunt, who made some creditable surveys of the more important harbors and the most frequented and dangerous portions of the Atlantic Coast, and published charts and a 'Coast Pilot,' which became the standard authority. It is true that as early as 1807 an effort was made to organize a national coast survey, but it failed, and the organization was not accomplished until 1832. No provision whatever was made for mitigating the distresses and horrors of actual shipwreck until several years later.

"Our merchants and ship-owners were equally slow to appreciate the importance of obtaining correct nautical information and to perceive the necessity of providing means for alleviating the hardships of navigation. They organized few undertakings for either purpose, and, indeed, the backwardness of the Government is in a measure chargeable to their indifference.

"Our country has doubtless maintained its full share of humane and benevolent organizations throughout its existence; but few of them have devoted special efforts to the prevention of loss of life and of suffering at sea, while the resources and exertions of most of them have entirely sought other channels of usefulness. The sturdy fishermen and wreckers living along the coast, however, usually gave their first efforts to the saving of life from the shipwrecked vessels cast upon their shores, and often imperiled their lives in rescuing passengers and crews.

"The occurrence of frequent and melancholy disasters at length awakened the Government to the duty and necessity of action, and one important step after another was taken in making provision for the greater security of life and property at sea. Generally, each successive measure was prosecuted with vigor and with advantageous results."

The annual report of the Light House Board to the Secretary of the Treasury of the United States for the fiscal year ending 1876 revealed that there were 434 lighted aids to navigation on the east coast of the U. S. and of these, 385 were lighthouses. There were 3,449 other aids consisting of 27 fog signals, 372 day beacons and 2,616 buoys. Clearly the apathy of the early days had disappeared. These aids to navigation were indeed an improvement but the storms continued to take their toll of shipwrecks. The perils of the sea were great and the violence of a shipwreck could break the spirit of the toughest sailor. The winter of 1877-1878 saw two tragic wrecks on the shores of North Carolina's outer banks. On November 24, 1877, the U.S. Navy steamer *Huron* was hit by gale winds about 1 a.m. and came ashore near Nags Head. The vessel became a total wreck and of a crew of 132 persons on board, 98 perished in the storm tossed waters off Cape Hatteras. On January 29, 1878, the steamer *Metropolis,* which had sailed from Philadelphia for Brazil, came ashore near Currituck Beach and was pounded to pieces by heavy surf. Of the 245 persons on board, 85 were lost.

The reports were not always bad however, the noted Joshua James was reputed to be the "Greatest Lifesaver off all time". He was a steadfast volunteer in the Massachusetts Humane Society for sixty years in the Hull-Nantasket area. He saved over one thousand lives during his career and in 1888 received the coveted gold medal from the U.S. Life Saving Service for an unforgettable rescue. James, along with his crew of volunteers, rescued twenty-nine persons from five different stranded vessels off the shores of Nantasket on November 25 and 26, 1888. A rescue which miraculously was carried out without the loss or serious injury to any of his crew or of the shipwrecked sailors he was able to save. His was a career of dedication to the principals of devotion to duty. His death was as dramatic as his life had been. On March 19, 1902, at the age of 76, while drilling his men with the lifeboat, he dropped dead of heart failure on the beach.

Death on Economy. Uncle Sam: "I suppose I must spend a little on Life-saving Service, Life-boat Stations, Life-Boats, Surf-Boats, etcetera; but it is too bad to be obliged to waste so much money."

On November 24, 1877, the U.S. Naval Steamer *Huron* was wrecked on the outer banks of North Carolina, with the loss of 98 men. Some time later, Harpers Weekly published a cartoon about the tightwad Uncle Sam and his reluctance to spend money on the Life Saving Service. *Reproduced from Harpers Weekly.*

Above: Because of an error in navigation, the steamer *Atlantic* ran up on the rocks near Mars Head, south of Halifax, Nova Scotia on April 1, 1873. The accident happened at night and 562 lives were lost, mostly women and children. The depiction of the disaster is by Currier and Ives. **Below:** The French steamer *Amerique* came ashore in a storm at Seabright, New Jersey on January 7, 1877. Three men were lost when a boat was launched from the ship and tipped over in heavy surf. The Life-savers removed one hundred passengers and crew from the steamer using the life car rigged on a hawser. The steamer lay on the beach until the morning of April 10th when she was pulled off by the Coast Wrecking Company and towed to New York. *Photos courtesy of the Mariners Museum, Newport News, Va.*

The bark *W.F. Marshall* went ashore on the south side of Nantucket Island on March 9, 1877 in thick fog. Sixteen persons were assisted ashore by the Life Savers. The bark was a total loss. *Photo from the collection of Paul C. Morris, Nantucket, Mass.*

Above: The *Altoona*, a small two masted schooner out of Boston, Mass., was wrecked during a severe storm at Cape Hatteras, North Carolina, on October 22, 1878. Her crew of seven was saved along with part of her cargo. The hull washed out in November 1962 and became a tourist attraction. *Photo courtesy of the Mariners Museum, Newport News, Va.* **Below:** An aerial view of the *Altoona* hull. In the photograph, there is a beach buggy just to the left of the wreck and people walking on the shore. This area is just south of the Cape Hatteras Lighthouse. *Photo courtesy of the Cape Hatteras National Seashore.*

The schooner *Lewis King* of Ellsworth, Maine went ashore in stormy weather at Montauk Point, Long Island, New York on December 18, 1887. The six crewmen and one passenger dropped to the beach from the jibboom and walked to the Life Saving station at Ditch Plain. Many salvage attempts were made but the vessel was ultimately lost because of the stranding. *Photo from the collection of Paul C. Morris, Nantucket, Mass.*

Above: The steamer *Arizona* rammed an iceberg outside Newfoundland shortly after nine p.m. on November 7, 1879 while on a crossing to Europe. She hit the berg head-on and sent everyone sprawling on the decks. No one was injured and the ship went into St. John harbor for repairs. *Photo courtesy of the Naval Historical Museum, Washington, D.C.* **Below:** The Life-savers of the Massachusetts Humane Society pose on the life-boat Nantasket, beside the breeches buoy apparatus. During the storm of November 25-26, 1888, Joshua James and his crew saved a total of 29 men from five different shipwrecks in Hull, Massachusetts using the breeches buoy and life-boats. *Photo from the collection of Richard M. Boonisar.*

Above: The wreckage of the *Gertrude Abbott* ashore north of Toddy Rocks. Eight men were rescued in a lifeboat by Joshua James and his crew. The lifeboat was wrecked on the rocks during the return trip to shore but all aboard made it safely to the beach. *Photo courtesy of the Mariners Museum, Newport News, Virginia.* **Below:** The three masted schooner *H.C. Higginson* stranded near Nantasket Beach at 8 p.m. on November 25, 1888, in a northeast gale. The Massachusetts Humane Society crew in the lifeboat Nantasket rescued the five surviving crewmen. This vessel was later towed to port in a damaged condition. *Photo from the collection of Richard M. Boonisar.*

Above: The three masted schooner *Mattie E. Eaton* came ashore at Nantasket Beach during the gale of 1888. This vessel washed up high and dry on shore and no assistance was required of the life savers to aid the crew. They stepped ashore at low tide. **Below:** The remains of the three masted schooner *Cox and Green* ashore north of Toddy Rocks in Hull, Massachusetts. Nine men were rescued by Joshua James and his crew of Humane society life savers using the breeches buoy from shore. *Photos courtesy of the Mariners Museum, Newport News, Virginia.*

The palatial steamer *Bristol*, one of the grand steamers of the Fall River Line, burned at her pier in Newport, Rhode Island on the night of December 30, 1888. She caught fire from fat boiling over in the galley. The ship was consumed by the flames. *Photos courtesy of the Mariners Museum, Newport News, Virginia.*

Above: On March 30, 1889, the steamship *City of Savannah* ran into the three masted schooner *Lester A. Lewis* off Sandy Hook Lightship in a snowstorm. Forty-six year old Captain Hatch of the schooner was killed when the steamer cut through his cabin and sheered off the entire port stern quarter of the vessel. The schooner stayed afloat on her cargo of lumber. She was later placed in a drydock and repaired. *Photo courtesy of the Mariners Museum, Newport News, Virginia.* **Below:** On April 7, 1889, a spring storm wrecked forty ships between Cape Henry, Virginia, and Cape Hatteras, North Carolina. The four masted schooner *Benjamin F. Poole* stranded on Virginia Beach. The crew was brought ashore by Life-savers using the breeches buoy. The vessel lay on the beach for seventeen months until another storm enabled wreckers to refloat her. She was in service until 1914. While on an ocean voyage from Wilmington, Delaware, around the DelMarVa peninsula to Baltimore, Maryland, she she went missing with a crew of eight. *Photo from the collection of Frank E. Claes*

The three masted schooner *James T. Maxwell, Jr.*, badly damaged in a storm was abandoned by her crew sixty miles east of Virginia in November, 1911. A U.S. Revenue Cutter found her and towed the vessel to port. *Photo courtesy of Capt. W.J.L. Parker, U.S.C.G. (Ret.)*

CHAPTER TWO

Alexander Hamilton was instrumental in establishing the United States Revenue Cutter Service. In 1790, he requested funds from Congress for ten ships to help implement the laws of our fledgling nation against smuggling in order to collect tariffs for the U.S. Treasury. In addition to the enforcement duties, the cutters began winter cruises in 1831 giving aid to ships in distress on the high seas. Their primary purpose was to save lives but they also helped to preserve personal property and to save cargoes of wrecked vessels. Wooden sailing vessels were always at the mercy of wind and sea. Frequently, storms dismasted square riggers and schooners. The crews often had to abandon their vessels at sea and the ship continued to float on, a derelict, drifting aimlessly with the ocean currents.

From the late 19th to the early 20th centuries, these derelicts, their decks awash, constituted a menace to other vessels at sea. The Revenue Cutter Service was charged with hunting them down and destroying them. Several were towed into port for disposal. The greatest danger posed by the derelicts was to lay in the path of another vessel underway at night or in fog where they could not be seen. Many times this would aggravate the situation. If the derelict was rammed by another wooden vessel, another derelict resulted.

At the end of the 19th century, the Atlantic ocean was scattered with hundreds of floating derelicts. Many became water-logged and finally sank while others seemed to go on and on. The three masted schooner *Alma Cummings* was abandoned off Virginia in February, 1895. A year later the vessel was reported to be still afloat 800 miles off the Cape Verdes Islands with her decks awash. In August of 1896, she finally washed ashore near Panama after an uncharted voyage of hundreds of miles. The wrecks continued well into the 20th century. The schooner *Warren Adams* was abandoned on December 27, 1914 at 33-25N and 75-53W and was picked up two days later by the Revenue Cutter *Itasca* at 35-17N and 74-58W, a drift of 113.5 miles in two days. She was towed into Newport News, Virginia and turned over to her owners.

TransAtlantic liners logged sightings of derelicts and reported them to the U.S. Navy's Hydrographic Office in Washington, D.C. These reports were charted and patterns of drift were noted. All factors were registered in the reports to determine the effects of drift with or without masts. Bulletins on derelicts and their drift patterns were issued each week to warn mariners of the locations. Vessels with masts standing were affected by winds as well as currents while hulls turned bottom up would meander and pretty much follow the ocean currents.

After 1900, the number of derelicts declined as more iron and steel ships were built to replace the wooden vessels. When the iron steamers were abandoned, they were usually sinking and were not destined to become derelicts. After the wireless radio was installed aboard ships, the task of locating and destroying the derelicts was made easier for the Revenue Cutter Service. The early trajectories charted by the Navy's Hydrographic office were recently studied by modern oceanographers plotting the north Atlantic surface currents. They compared the 19th century reports with today's scientific data and it was found that the early derelict bulletins were considered more reliable than the contemporary findings which used drifting buoys emitting radio beacons to trace the drift patterns. The large mass of a ship's hull would probably be affected more by the ocean currents than that of a small buoy.

Above: The three masted schooner *Alice Murphy* ran into a storm off Cape Hatteras on April 3, 1915. The crew were rescued but the vessel foundered and floated on her cargo of lumber. The stern appears to have gone through a fire as the mizzen mast is gone. Surface currents carried the hull out into the Atlantic. She was last spotted six hundred miles east of New York in the Gulf Stream headed east. *Photo courtesy of Capt. W.J.L. Parker, U.S.C.G. (Ret.)* **Below:** The schooner *James M.W. Hall* sailed from Charleston, South Carolina for Boston on January 5, 1922 with a cargo of 516,567 feet of kiln dried lumber. The vessel met heavy gales and rough seas. On January 10, the schooner sprung a leak and filled until her decks were awash. The crew battled to save their vessel until January 15th when they were rescued by the steamer *West Cannon,* underway from Gibraltar for New York. The derelict, floating on her cargo, was later picked up by the Coast Guard Cutter *Seneca* and towed to New York. *Photos courtesy of U.S. Coast Guard, Washington, D.C.*

Some of the derelicts set records for longevity. The 120 foot schooner *Fannie E. Wolston* was launched in 1882 in Bath, Maine. She was abandoned on October 1891, off Cape Hatteras and began a long unmanned voyage in the Gulf Stream. In June 1892, she was sighted half way across the Atlantic. In January 1893, she had turned around and headed south in the mid-Atlantic. At this point, she was plotted over one thousand miles from her original position when abandoned. The currents carried her in an erratic pattern and she was last sighted off the coast of Georgia after covering a distance of over 7,000 miles. She seemed destined to sail on forever like the legendary *Flying Dutchman* floating along, never able to reach her home port.

Perhaps the oldest and best known sailor's superstition is that of the *Flying Dutchman*. There are different versions but basically its about a mythical Dutch vessel, under Captain Vanderdecken who is forever struggling to reach his home port of Batavia. His labors are in vain because of his defiance of the Almighty. It was considered a bad omen to sight the *Flying Dutchman*. He usually showed up just before a vessel foundered or ran aground on a lee shore. One of the legends located the Dutch vessel off the Cape of Good Hope at the southern tip of Africa with her Captain dressed in yellow wearing a night cap, smoking a short pipe, and was jealous of mariners who succeed in doubling the Cape and tried to frighten them away.

There are various other superstitions and marine folklore, born in the age of sail and passed from father to son. Some have established customs still in use today. They still break a bottle of wine on the bow of a ship when she is launched to ward off evil spirits. A few of the lesser known taboos were: Never sail on Friday, never use blue paint and knock on wood to continue good fortune. Red sky at night, sailors delight. Red sky in the morning, sailors take warning. One only needs a keen weather eye to solve the meaning of this ditty. Sea serpents were reported to have been seen at various times by sailors on the high seas. The description varied in proportion to the degree of inebriation. Sometimes five hundred feet long with two or three heads breathing fire and smoke. These apparitions have been rumored but none ever proved to exist. In Scotland, scientists have been pursuing the Loch Ness monster for years without success. Some of the sightings are considered to be mirages. Sometimes when conditions are right, at sea, one might see another ship in the distance upside-down. This sometimes happens when there is a low lying fog bank or mist nearby creating the illusion.

In 1894, one such illusion was sighted off Cape Hatteras by officers and men of the steamship *El Norte* while on a passage from New Orleans to New York City. Chief Officer Benson reported that on March 18th the vessel was passing the North Carolina coast with a mild swell running from the northeast. There was no wind and a thin haze was seen on the horizon. At sunrise the illusion occurred in the west. There was a fleet of sailing vessels, right side up sailing atop the mist. Entire hulls were visible and Benson reported counting twenty-eight different ships with all sails set. He reported a low lying bank of fog under the vessels and it remained there for two hours. When the sun rose higher in the sky it dispersed the fog and the phantom fleet faded out of sight. The phenomenon could be attributed to a double layer of fog lying off shore under a high pressure area where there was no wind to disperse the mist. The fact that a mild swell was reported and no wind would support this theory. There have been stranger sightings at sea by mariners of good reputations, not given to imbibing in strong spirits.

Above: The fishing schooner *Mary F. Kelly* was anchored off Manasquan Beach, New Jersey on the night of August 24, 1893, when a violent storm bore down on her snapping her cable and driving her ashore. When she hit the outer bar, a huge wave washed over her deck and carried three men, including the Captain, to their deaths. Seven men were saved by the Life Savers but another man was later found dead in the cabin of the schooner. *Photo courtesy of the Mariners Museum, Newport News, Virginia.* **Below:** On the afternoon of October 25, 1893, the schooner *Horatio L. Baker,* while under tow of the tug *A.W.Chesterton,* was in a collision with the schooner *John S. Ames* as she was passing Bug Light outside Boston harbor. The *Horatio L. Baker* lost her foremast and her mainmast was broken. She was cut to the waterline amidships on the starboard side. The *John S. Ames* had her jibboom and headgear carried away and suffered damage to the stem. The accident was caused by a strong ebb tide which forced the two schooners together. Both vessels were later repaired. *Photo by Nathaniel Stebbins, courtesy of the Society for the Preservation of New England Antiquities, Boston, Mass.*

THE JASON

The full rigged ship *Jason* from Calcutta for Boston was caught in a northeast gale and snowstorm off Cape Cod on December 5, 1893. The vessel was wrecked near Pamet River in Truro. From a crew of 25 men, only one survived when he was washed ashore clinging to a bale of jute, the cargo of the wrecked vessel. Life Savers were on the beach all night looking for survivors but the bodies of only 20 of her crew were found. *Photo by Henry K. Cummings, Orleans, Massachusetts.* -The *JASON* lies at approximately 42-00.5N, 70-00.9W

The introduction of the U.S. Life Saving Service report for the year ending June 30,1894 carries the report of the loss of the *Jason* on the backside shore of Cape Cod. A full rigged ship of 1,512 gross tons out of Greenock, Scotland, Captain McMillan, bound from Calcutta, India to Boston, Massachusetts. The vessel carried a cargo of 10,000 bales of jute and a crew of 25 men. Thick weather prevailed for several days off the coast of Massachusetts and the Captain was unable to determine his position. While 100 miles off the coast he set his course to the westward to raise a landmark. When the vessel approached Cape Cod the wind was blowing a gale from the northeast with thickening weather and rain. The falling temperatures soon turned the rain to sleet and snow. The vessel was spotted by the patrol of the Nauset Life Saving Station and word was sent to other stations along the shore to be on the lookout for the imperiled ship. Shortly after seven in the evening the *Jason* struck the outer bar, about a mile north of the Pamet River station. Crewmen aboard the ship attempted to launch their boats but all were washed overboard by the tremendous seas breaking over the stranded vessel. Wreckage washed ashore and lifesavers on the beach succeeded in saving only one man, Samuel J. Evans, who floated ashore on a bale of jute. The bodies of 20 of the crew were found and buried in the cemetery vault in Wellfleet. Total loss of the ship and cargo was listed as $119,420.

THE SOMMERS N. SMITH

It was just one of those days better forgotten. A launching on Memorial Day in 1896 was not one to enhance the record books at the Newport News Shipbuilding and Dry Dock Company. The *Sommers N. Smith*, a steam pilot boat was launched with improperly placed ballast. The hull rolled over and sank on her beam ends. She was later raised. After some drydock repairs and new paint, the vessel was launched again. The vessel did long service in Florida waters. *Photos courtesy of the Mariners Museum, Newport News, Virginia.*

22

A delightful occasion was a double launch day at the shipyard. It was Memorial Day in 1896 at the Newport News Shipbuilding and Drydock Company. Hull #17, was the *Sommers N. Smith* and, along with hull # 20, the *Margaret* a side-wheeler, were the vessels launched that day. The *Smith* was the first to be launched. The steel steam pilot boat, 118 feet long, was scheduled for service in Florida and much of her deck structure had been completed. This, along with improperly placed ballast resulted in the hull flipping over upon launching. The ports were open and she began to take on water immediately. She sank on her port beam ends. It must have been embarrassing at the time and more than one of those launching aboard must have got a dunking. A valuable lesson in launching was probably learned. The *Sommers N. Smith* drifted out of the way and the *Margaret* was launched successfully soon after. The *Smith* was none the worse for wear however and was later raised. She was put into drydock and cleaned out. She proved to be a serviceable vessel in spite of her inauspicious beginning.

Above: The steamer *J. Putnam Bradlee* was wrecked on Goal Rock in the Weir River near Nantasket, Massachusetts on September 12, 1894. In what the Boston Globe described as "a merry party of insurance delegates on an outing to Nantasket." The vessel piled up on the rock in mid-afternoon. The party halted temporarily until another steamer came along and removed the 250 passengers. The vessel settled in the water hung up on the rock. The paper also reported that the party proceeded to Nantasket and had a good time. During the festivities, a band was playing a loud catchy tune and the Captain of the steamer blamed the accident on the music as the engineer could not hear the bells to slow the vessel down when she approached the rocks. **Below:** On September 17th the ship was raised and towed to Boston for repairs. The method of salvage employed is interesting. Four salvage barges are placed around the steamer. At low tide, cables are made fast to the hull. When the tide comes in, the ship is raised off the bottom. It is then moved to a drydock for repairs. *Photos from the Author's collection.*

The recorded maritime history of the east coast details many storms where there is a high incident of vessels and people lost. Killer gales were recorded in 1839, 1851, 1873 and 1886. But none was to compare with the great hurricane of November of 1898. This storm is commonly referred to as the Portland Gale, after the steamer *Portland* which was lost at sea with all hands. The storm was described in the annual report of the U.S. Lifesaving Service as:

"A memorable cyclonic tempest which struck the New England coast, especially the south shore of Massachusetts Bay, in the evening of Saturday, November 26, 1898, and raged with almost unprecedented violence for twenty-four hours, and with gradually abating force for twelve hours longer-two nights and one day.

"Probably this storm will longest be remembered and generally designated as that which destroyed the steamer *Portland* with all her crew and passengers, estimated as numbering between one hundred fifty and two hundred people. No such appalling calamity has occurred anywhere near by the coasts of the United States, or on the shore, for almost half a century, and it is doubtful whether there has been within the same period a coast storm of such Titanic power.

"When the *Portland* steamed away from her pier in Boston Harbor, at about seven in the evening, scores of sailing vessels between Gay Head and Cape Ann were hunting for harbors of refuge. Forty took shelter in Vineyard Haven, of which number more than half suffered injury. Many found anchorage in Provincetown and Gloucester, while others were crowding on every sail they could safely carry to reach port. Those already there passed additional stout lines to the dock or dropped another trustworthy anchor."

The storm wrecked more ships than any other in the history of New England. It is estimated that over 150 vessels were lost, both in the harbors and at sea. Many were never heard from. Miles of coastline from Buzzards Bay to Cape Ann were strewn with wreckage. A vessel was smashed against a house in Quincy. The physical appearance of the shore line was altered by the wind and waves. The snowfall was very deep. Telephone and telegraph lines were down all along the coastline. The wreckage from the steamer *Portland* washed ashore along the entire backside of Cape Cod. Because the storm had interrupted all communications, there was difficulty in getting the news to Boston. It was decided to send a wire to France over the trans-Atlantic French cable from the station in Orleans. From there the story was wired back to New York over another cable. The news was then telegraphed to Boston.

The cost in dollar value of this storm was enormous. It was estimated that over 450 persons lost their lives as a result of the hurricane. The damage in the town of Hull, Massachusetts which includes Nantasket Beach was estimated to be in excess of $200,000. If that was calculated in today's inflated values it would run into the millions of dollars. The Life Saving Service report concludes the story on the storm:

"Against such an indescribable pandemonium of wind and sea as the fragmentary review suggests, few craft, steam or sail, could successfully contend on a lee shore, and the deplorable consequence was that the coast, rocks, and islands from Gay Head to Cape Ann were strewn with wrecked or disabled vessels, while an uncertain but considerable number founded not far away at sea."

The great gale of November 26-27, 1898 is called the "Portland Gale" by New Englanders after the steamer *Portland* was lost with all hands during the storm. The photo above is a copy of a painting by Wallace Randall that hangs in the Marine Museum at Fall River, Massachusetts, it depicts the steamer at sea during the storm. It was estimated that approximately 175 persons lost their lives when the ship went down. The gale wrecked over 150 ships on the eastern seaboard. **Below:** The pilot boat *Columbia* was photographed ashore at Scituate, smashed against a beach cottage, The crew of five men were lost in the storm. The schooner lay on the beach and was later converted into a summer cottage. *Photo courtesy of the Smithsonian Institution, Washington, D.C.*

Above The schooner *Edgar S. Foster* was wrecked a half mile from the Brant Rock Life Saving Station near Plymouth, Massachusetts, during the Portland Gale. The crew of eight men reached the shore unaided and went to a vacant cottage nearby to get out of the storm. **Below** The damage to waterfront property during the great gale of 1898 was extensive. This photograph at Nantasket shows beach cottages moved off their foundations and broken apart. *Photos courtesy of Richard M. Boonisar.*

THE BARKENTINE PRISCILLA

The *Priscilla* an American barkentine of 643 tons was on a voyage from Baltimore, Maryland to Rio de Janeiro, Brazil with general cargo under the command of Captain Benjamin E. Springsteen. On August 17, 1899, the vessel was caught in a hurricane east of Cape Hatteras, North Carolina and cast ashore three miles south of the Gull Shoal life saving station. At 3 a.m., Surfman Rasmus S. Midgett was on his regular south patrol on horseback when he discovered the shipwreck. The vessel had broken into three pieces and ten men were clinging to a piece of the wreckage. Four persons had been lost in the raging seas prior to the ship coming ashore. Surfman Midgett rescued the ten persons single handed by racing into the surf and assisting each person ashore. When all of the men were safe he rode back for help and the rescued crewmen were brought to the station. The wounded were treated and the bodies of those lost were recovered. For his heroism Surfman Midgett was awarded the Gold Life Saving Medal on October 18, 1899.

The violence of a hurricane was tragically exhibited on August 17, 1899 when the barkentine *Priscilla* was wrecked on Cape Hatteras, North Carolina. The ship struck the shoals and broke into pieces. The crew climbed into the rigging. Four persons were lost, including the Captain's wife and son. The life savers succeeded in saving ten crewmen out of the raging surf on the outer banks. *Photos from the North Carolina Collection at the U.N.C. Library, Chapel Hill.*

Above: The schooner *Falmouth* lay at anchor off Rehoboth Beach, Delaware on the morning of October 31, 1899. The weather was stormy and the vessel dragged her anchors. She was driven on the beach by the heavy surf. Life Savers hauled the beach cart to the scene to effect a rescue of the crew but the sailors had dropped to the beach on a line over the side of the ship. The schooner was later refloated and she went back to sea. **Below:** During a bad storm on August 18, 1899, the Diamond Shoals lightship came ashore near the Creeds Hill Life Saving Station at Cape Hatteras, North Carolina. The surfmen landed the crew using the breeches buoy. The vessel lay on the beach for a couple of months before the Merritt Wrecking Company succeeded in refloating her. The ship was towed to Baltimore for repairs. *Photos courtesy of the Mariners Museum, Newport News, Virginia*

Above: The steamer *Gate City* of the Savannah Line was underway for Boston on February 8, 1900 when she ran aground in dense fog at Moriches, Long Island, N.Y. Life savers removed forty-eight persons from the wreck and wreckers salvaged part of her cargo but the vessel was a total loss. *Photo from the collection of Paul C. Morris.* **Below:** A number of survivors from a shipwreck were landed in a surfboat of the United States Life Saving Service. This scene was repeated often and thousands were rescued by these guardians of the shore. *Photo courtesy of the National Archives, Washington, D.C.*

Above: The four masted British ship *County of Edinburgh* ran aground near Squan Beach, New Jersey on February 12, 1900. Life savers assisted her crew and delivered messages to the wrecking company. The vessel was floated on the 25th of February and towed to New York. **Below:** A puzzling accident occurred in June, 1900 at the William Skinner & Son ship railway in Baltimore. The steamer *Hudson* capsized on the marine railway. The damages to ship and railway amounted to over twenty thousand dollars. The Merritt & Chapman Wrecking Company righted the ship at a cost of almost $10,000. The vessel went back to sea after the repairs had been made. *Photos courtesy of the Mariners Museum, Newport News, Virginia.*

The five masted schooner *Nathaniel T. Palmer* stranded at Long Beach, New Jersey at 3 a.m. on March 11, 1901 in thick weather and rough seas. Her crew of 12 men were landed by Life Savers using the breeches buoy. The vessel lay on the beach for a little over a week before it was refloated. The *Nathaniel T. Palmer* was built in 1898 in Bath, Maine and her gross tonnage was 2,440. *Photo from the collection of Paul C Morris, Nantucket, Mass.*

Above: The four masted steel hulled bark *Sindia* was fighting heavy weather on the night of December 15, 1901 off the coast of New Jersey when she stranded on the beach at Ocean City. Life Savers removed her crew by surfboat. Two days later she filled with water and was abandoned to wreckers. The *Sindia* was bound from Kobe, Japan to New York City with a cargo of Japanese porcelain, silk, camphor and linseed oil. Wreckers succeeded in salvaging part of her cargo but much of it is still buried under the sands off Ocean City. The loss was valued at $249,000. **Below:** Along the New Jersey shore the Life Savers used the Jersey skiff to work the shipwrecks. *Photos from the collection of Paul C. Morris, Nantucket, Mass.*

CHAPTER THREE

The east coast of the United States is diverse with each mile between Eastport, Maine and Key West, Florida. The weather off shore ranges from ideal to dangerous. No one location is storm free but the southern shores enjoy better average conditions over a long period of time. Beginning at the northern point, the coasts of Maine and New Hampshire are rocky. They are interrupted by rivers and islands forming numerous sounds and bays. These areas have many reefs, points and headlands. Around these are submerged rocks to snare the mariner and trap his vessel. Conversely, the bays and inlets offer several harbors of refuge to enable the vessels a shelter in time of adverse weather.

Massachusetts extends out into the Atlantic at two points. Cape Ann and Cape Cod. Cape Ann extends fifteen miles out from the coast. It is irregular and bordered by dangerous ledges. Between Cape Ann and Cape Cod is the Massachusetts Bay which is the entrance to the port of Boston. The channel to this city is dotted with islands and the mariner must exercise caution when entering the port. Cape Cod projects forty miles out into the Atlantic ocean and then bends upwards for another thirty miles with rows of shifting sand bars near the shore line which are moved by the wind, currents and surf. Thousands of ships have met their fate here on the ocean side and some of their bones still lie in the surf wash.

South of Cape Cod lie the islands of Martha's Vineyard and Nantucket. Between the Cape and Islands there are numerous shoals and reefs. On the floor of Nantucket and Vineyard sounds lie the bottoms of countless schooners which ran aground while going "over the shoals". On May 16,1909, the five masted schooner *Jennie French Potter* was underway in Nantucket Sound when the wind died and the current carried her on to Half Moon Shoal where she grounded. The vessel was laden with coal and when the tide dropped, she opened her seams and filled with water. It was a general practice that when passing over the shoals, if the wind died, a wise Captain dropped his anchor.

Between Gay Head, the western end of Martha's Vineyard, and Montauk Point, the eastern tip of Long Island, New York, lies Rhode Island, open to the sea and exposed to the violence of southerly storms. Ship traffic moves on both sides of Long Island towards New York City and the coastline is dotted with shattered hulls of wrecks from years gone by. The coast from Long Island to Cape Fear is six-hundred miles of beach except for New York, Delaware and Chesapeake Bays. There are rivers, islands and inlets where the outer shore is separated from the mainland by long narrow bays except in North Carolina where the intervening waters expand into Albemarle and Pamlico Sounds. There are few navigable inlets along this foreboding shoreline as storms open and close them frequently.

Cape Hatteras extends out into the Atlantic with shoals and reefs all along its length. Weather contributes to many wrecks on this stretch of beach. The Gulf Stream meanders by, sometimes within twenty miles of shore. The merging of the warm and cold currents produces frequent clashes of air masses resulting in small storms which are extremely hazardous to shipping. Most mariners try to stay a hundred miles east of Cape Hatteras and the dreaded Diamond Shoals. The distance between Cape Henry in Virginia and Cape Lookout, North Carolina is about 200 miles. The U.S. Life Saving Service maintained no less than thirty-two lifeboat stations on this stretch of beach because of the incessant wrecks that piled up on the coastline.

The coast swings westward from Cape Lookout on its line along the bays and sounds of South Carolina past the port of Charleston down to the states of Georgia and Florida. The outer coastline of Florida is almost unbroken for nearly 500 miles and is the wrecking ground for vessels leaving the Gulf of Mexico. During the fall months, this area is subject to tropical hurricanes. In the winter, squalls and rainstorms are usually the worst the mariner has to endure. The rest of the year, tropical conditions prevail.

Above: Three liners of the North German Lloyd lines were lost to fire at their docks at Hoboken, New Jersey on June 30, 1900. The *SS Bremen*, above and the *SS Seale* and the *SS Main* were lost in the blaze. The fire started on the piers and spread rapidly engulfing the three ships. *Photo courtesy of the Mariners Museum, Newport News, Virginia.* **Below:** The *Main* and the *Bremen* were beached at Hoboken after the fires were extinguished. It was estimated that nearly 400 persons died in the conflagration. *Photo courtesy of the Mystic Seaport, Mystic Connecticut.*

Along this whole perplexing coastline the U.S. Life Saving Service was charged with saving lives and property imperiled by the seas. They were proficient in their work and improved their techniques in life-saving, using new ideas and apparatus. In the early 1900's, the most welcome addition to their equipment was the motor lifeboat. The new 36-foot, self-righting and self-bailing boat was driven by a gasoline engine. This relieved the men of long backbreaking duty at the oars on extended trips in the ocean searching for survivors of a shipwreck. One of the most beneficial safety improvements in the maritime field was the development of the wireless radio. In 1903, Guglielmo Marconi was sending messages across the Atlantic. This invention was to become the most valuable addition to marine safety since the steam engine.

During the early 1900's many tragic accidents occurred along the coast. A major conflagration occurred at the North German Lloyd docks in Hoboken, New Jersey on June 30, 1900. The fire started in stored bales of cotton on pier 3 and spread rapidly over a quarter mile of waterfront involving four ocean liners and a score of smaller craft in the area. The loss of life resulting from the fire was estimated at about 400 persons. The exact number was never determined as many persons were lost overboard and many bodies were never recovered. The fire was fed by stored materials on the piers and fanned by brisk winds at the time. The new German liner *Kaiser Wilhelm der Grosse* left the pier at once to avoid the flames but two hundred feet of her decks and woodwork were burned. Three other vessels, the *Saale, Main* and *Bremen* were badly charred. The fire began at about four in the afternoon and it took fire-fighters six hours to bring it under control. The loss to the North German Lloyd line was estimated to be about $2,250,000. A large number of lighters, canalboats and barges along with their cargoes were consumed in the flames. The piers, cargoes and property that were lost were valued at six million dollars. The steamer *Saale* which had a cargo of copper, cotton and general merchandise was grounded just north of Ellis Island. The *Main*, which was almost totally destroyed in the fire and the *Bremen* were beached near Weehawken, New Jersey.

One of the worst marine disasters occurred on June 15, 1904 when the steamer *General Slocum* burned, with the loss of 1031 persons near Hell Gate, New York City. Most of those who died were women and children. The ship was on an annual excursion cruise for the Sunday school classes of St. Marks German Lutheran Church. The disaster was caused by an explosion in the cookstove. The flames spread among the dry wooden beams of the ship covered with many coats of old paint, fanned by a brisk head-on breeze. Soon the entire ship was an inferno, and hysteria spread among the passengers. The panic drove people over the side to escape the flames. Most of these drowned or were crushed under the churning paddle wheels. The Captain became alarmed and steered his ship full speed, up the river to a remote area off North Brother Island killing scores in his flight.

Late on the night of February 11, 1907 in Block Island sound with the air temperature at three degrees F, the schooner *Harry Knowlton*, sailing with a fair wind rammed the passenger steamer *Larchmont* with 150 passengers and a crew of 35. The schooner struck the steamer amidships forward of the paddlewheel. Both vessels suffered fatal damage. The schooner was grounded near Block Island and was a total loss. Her crew of seven landed in the ship's boat. The *Larchmont* sank in twelve minutes, carrying half of the people aboard her down as she sank. The other half nearly all froze to death in the open lifeboats. The boats came ashore on Block Island the next day, and of the nearly 200 persons on board the steamer, only 20 survived, and three of those died later. There was little time to fire rockets or other distress signals and this accounted for the high death rate. It was a clear night and many could have been saved as the accident occurred only four miles off shore from the Life-saving crews on Block Island.

Above: A collision in dense fog in Long Island sound resulted in the deaths of six people aboard the Fall River liner *Plymouth* early in the morning of March 20, 1903. The only passenger ever lost on a Fall River liner in ninety years of service was Mr. G.H. Marsten of Paterson, New Jersey.**Below:** The other steamer, the *City of Taunton*, a freight boat for the Fall River Line ripped off her bow in the collision. Extensive damage was done to the *Plymouth* and five of her crewmen were killed. The liner went into New London to get medical attention for the injured passengers. Damage was set at $28,000 to the steamer *Plymouth. Photos courtesy of the Mariners Museum, Newport News, Virginia.*

Above: On March 21, 1903, during a stiff south wind and in rough seas, the American schooner *John F. Kranz* ran aground at Mantoloking, New Jersey. The life-savers launched a life boat and removed her crew of eight men. The vessel was a total loss but part of her cargo of valuable logwood was saved. *Photo from the collection of Paul C. Morris, Nantucket, Mass.*
Below: On the afternoon of December 26, 1903 a blinding snowstorm reduced visibility in Boston harbor to a few feet and the steamer *Admiral Dewey* was in collision with the steamship *Kiowa* while she was anchored outside the harbor. The *Kiowa* sank near the channel and her crew was removed by a city tug and brought to shore. The *Kiowa* had a full cargo of lumber, cotton, naval stores, iron and general merchandise. The wreckage was never raised and her remains still lie, a mile south of Boston Light. *Photo from the collection of Richard M. Boonisar.*

Above: On February 19, 1904, the downeaster *Henry B. Hyde* broke loose from a towboat in gale winds and went ashore south of Cape Henry, Virginia. Life-savers rescued her crew of 13 via the breeches buoy. The vessel could not be refloated and four wreckers were working on her salvage when another storm hit the beach on June 10th. Again the Life-savers set up the apparatus and landed the people. The loss of the ship was estimated at $50,000. **Below:** It is a rare occurrence when a ship and a train collide but it happened on June 20, 1904 in Laurel, Delaware, when the Delaware Railroad's Norfolk Express went through an open draw and plunged down into the river just as the schooner *Golden Gate* was passing under the open drawbridge. The crew of the vessel all jumped into the river and swam ashore. The engineer of the train lost his life in the accident but there were no other injuries. The baggage master turned out to be the hero of the day when he crawled under the moving train to uncouple the cars with the passengers aboard. The schooner was a total loss but the engine was recovered and repaired. *Photos courtesy of the Mariners Museum, Newport, News, Virginia.*

Above: On June 15, 1904, the *General Slocum* steamed away from the third street dock in New York City, with a full load of people headed for a Sunday school picnic. There were 1,358 passengers aboard, most of whom were children. A fire broke out in the galley and could not be controlled. In one of histories worst maritime disasters, 1,031 lives were lost in the fire. Later, investigations revealed that violations of safety regulations and substandard fire fighting equipment were the causes of the disaster. *Photo courtesy of the Steamship Historical Society of America.* **Below:** The Delaware built four masted schooner *James Judge* came ashore at Palm Beach, Florida on October 19, 1904 and sanded in on the beach. The vessel was listed in the registry as lost but it would appear by the photograph that someone had a fine beach home, right on the ocean. *Photo courtesy of the Mariners Museum, Newport News, Va.*

Above: The Italian steamer *Vincenzo Bonanno* was steaming through dense fog on the evening of June 17, 1906 when she stranded just off Fire Island, New York, 150 yards from shore. The Life-savers from the Point of Woods station rigged the breeches buoy apparatus and stood by. The steamer was re-floated ten days later and taken to New York City. *Photo by Anderson, courtesy of the Suffolk Marine Museum, West Sayville, N.Y.* **Below:** On January 14, 1907, the ship *Ruby*, while under tow, went aground at Fernandina Beach, Florida. The vessel carried a full load of lumber and could not be moved. She settled in the sand and was a total wreck but the cargo was salvaged. *Photo courtesy of the Mariners Museum, Newport News, Virginia.*

Above: On the evening of October 20, 1906, the steamer *George Farwell* was underway outside Cape Henry off the coast of Virginia, in a northeast gale, when she ran aground about 3/4 miles southeast of the Cape Henry Life Saving Station. The men of the station quickly rigged the breeches buoy and successfully landed the crew of 16 men from the stranded vessel. The ship had a $25,000 cargo of lumber on board, only part of which was saved. The vessel was a total loss. In the photograph, just off the stern of the *George Farwell* are the masts of the Italian bark *Antonio* which was wrecked on March 31, 1906, in the same location. Men of the Life-saving station rescued her crew of eleven men with the lifeboat. *Photo courtesy of the Mariners Museum, Newport News, Virginia.* **Below:** At the Virginia Beach Maritime Historical Museum in Virginia Beach, housed in the former Life Saving Station, is a portion of the engine from the steamer *George Farwell* on display. *Photo by William P. Quinn.*

In April 7, 1907, while on a voyage from New York City to Wiggins, South Carolina, the four masted schooner *Louis Bossert* stranded near Nags Head, North Carolina in thick weather. Life Savers rigged the breeches buoy and landed the crew of eight men and two lady passengers. The persons landed were sheltered at the Life Saving station for a few days and later went back aboard their vessel, which was re-floated on April 12th. *Photo courtesy of the Mariners Museum, Newport News, Virginia.*

Above: The small fishing schooner *Pythian* out of Gloucester, Massachusetts was driven ashore in a gale and sunk at Kittery Point, Maine, on February 1, 1908. The crew of thirteen men were all saved but the schooner was damaged. She was raised a few weeks later and towed to Gloucester where she was repaired. *Photo courtesy of Brewster Harding, Portland, Maine.* **Below** The steamer *Marion* burned in what is reported to be the worst maritime disaster in South Carolina. Twenty-six persons died when the fire got out of control. Her Captain rammed the vessel into a dock at Charleston to enable passengers to jump for their lives. The fire began at 5 a.m. on April 11, 1907, and everyone woke up to flames. After the vessel hit the dock the Captain ordered her scuttled in order to put out the fire. The hulk was raised and towed to a shipyard where the above photograph was made. Originally, she probably looked like the steamer *Lotta*, hauled out in the background. *Photo courtesy of Mrs Donald D. Sams, Charleston, S.C.*

45

Above: The White Star liner *Republic,* following the collision with the *Florida.* The ship has a large canvas patch on her side covering the hole caused by the accident on January 23, 1909. This vessel was taken in tow by the Revenue cutter *Gresham* but she sank before they could reach shoal waters. All hands aside from the six killed in the initial collision were saved. The *Republic* lies at approximately 40-25.5 N, and 69-40.0 W. *Photo copied from Harpers Weekly.* **Below:** The Italian liner *Florida* lost her bow in the accident, twenty-six miles southwest of Nantucket Island, off the coast of Massachusetts. This was reported as the first maritime disaster where the wireless radio played an important part in the rescue of persons at sea. *Photo courtesy of the Peabody Museum of Salem, Massachusetts.*

On January 23,1909, in dense fog 26 miles southwest of Nantucket Island the Italian liner *Florida* rammed into the side of the British steamer *Republic* ripping open the hull to the cold Atlantic. Six lives were lost but, more important, it was the first use of the new radio wireless to call for help. The collision bulkhead on the *Florida* held up but she lost thirty feet of her bow. The *Republic* was a doomed ship but the radio operator, Jack Binns, stood by his radio key tapping out the S O S messages to bring aid to the sinking vessel. The steamer *Baltic* arrived on scene and·rescued 1,650 passengers from the two ships, a vast undertaking using small boats at sea. The *Republic* was sinking and the Revenue cutter *Gresham* took her in tow for shoal water but she sank before they could save her. All hands but the six killed in the initial collision were saved. Jack Binns had transmitted more than 200 messages during the ordeal. He was lauded around the world. Unique was the magic of the new radio and its ability to save lives at sea in a disaster.

The Life Saving Service men who launched the lifeboats in the face of gale winds and treacherous seas were often the unsung heroes who rarely appeared in the headlines. Their rescue efforts were ordinarily carried out along deserted beaches where no one witnessed their courage. Circumstances were different however, on August 19, 1909 at Long Beach, Long Island, New York. The three masted schooner *Arlington*, fighting a gale, came ashore, 300 yards in front of the Nassau Hotel at about 4:30 a.m. The heavy seas smashed over her stern and made a clean breach over the vessel, driving her crew of nine out on the jibboom in the fore part of the vessel. The constant pounding of the waves broke open the vessel near the stern and she became a total wreck. Surfman Charles Helmcke from the Long Beach station spotted the schooner and sounded the alarm. The crew of the station immediately assembled at the scene and made several unsuccessful attempts to reach the vessel with the beach apparatus.

When the guests at the hotel heard the line gun fired, they gathered on the porch to cheer on the life-savers in the rescue attempt. When the life-savers failed to reach the schooner with the line throwing gun the onlookers became impatient. "Why don't you do something? Are you going to let them drown without making an effort?." At 8:30 a.m., after the tide had ebbed, the surfmen launched their boat with the aid of other lifesavers from the Point Lookout station. One man, Mans Pierson, fell off the bowsprit. He grabbed a small piece of wreckage floating nearby and was carried away by the current. The surf boat fought the heavy surf and managed to work out to where the men were clinging in the fore chains and then they dropped, one at a time into the water where they were picked up by the men in the boat. Eight wet survivors were brought ashore amid the cheers of the hotel guests.

Normally, shipwreck survivors are taken to the Life Saving Station and given medical attention, dry clothing and warm food. But when the lifeboat touched the beach, the men were surrounded by the hotel people and taken to a private suite where clothing, donated by guests, was distributed among the sailors. The hotel guests had taken up a collection and a purse of $500 was to be divided among the crewmen. The story had a happy ending the next day when Mans Pierson, the man who had fallen off the bowsprit and floated away on wreckage, was picked up by a fishing boat and brought ashore. He was given a share of the money donated by the hotel guests for the crew of the *Arlington*. In contrast, a major disaster occurred off Eastport, Maine when the steamer *Hestia* was lost when she ran up on a ledge. A bad compass was blamed for the accident that cost 35 lives. Life-savers at the Seal Cove Life Saving Station saved six survivors from the vessel but the rest had left in the ship's boat and were lost in the storm.

Above: The four masted schooner *Alice E. Clark* stranded on Coombs Ledge off Islesboro, Maine on the afternoon of July 1, 1909. The vessel was out of the channel when she ran up on the rock. The sharp ledge pierced the hull and she sank by the stern. She later broke up in a storm and was a total loss. Photo from the collection of *Paul C. Morris, Nantucket, Mass.*
Below: The U.S. Naval auxiliary training ship *Yankee* went aground on Spindle Rock in the western end of Buzzards Bay on September 23, 1908. She was raised in December but sank while being towed to New Bedford and was declared a total loss. *Photo Courtesy of Mystic Seaport Museum, Mystic, Connecticut.*

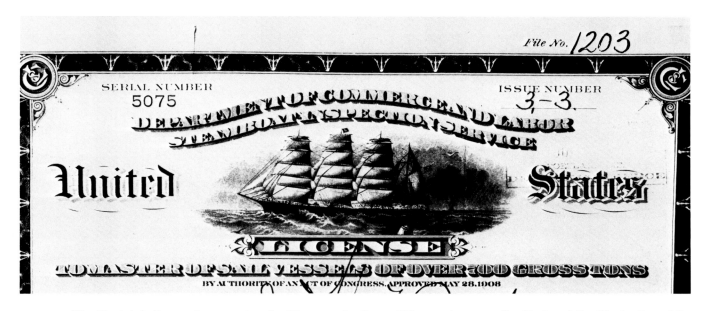

 File No. 1203

The Captain's license for a master of sailing vessels of over 700 gross tons proudly displayed the illustration of the Bath Maine built Shenendoah. *A close look will reveal the Sewall house flag with the "S" plainly visible atop the main mast.* Photo courtesy of the Maine Maritime Museum, Bath, Maine.

CHAPTER FOUR

The ships that sailed the world's oceans underwent a gradual change during the second half of the 19th century. The days of the wooden sailing ships were ending. Ultimately, with the arrival of the 20th century, iron and steel were predominant in new ship construction. The beautiful days of sail had passed by and the sight of a full rigged ship with all sails set, with the wind on her quarter and the bone in her teeth were almost gone. One of these, the *Shenandoah* was a four masted bark of 3,407 tons, launched in Bath, Maine on November 26, 1890. She was considered to be one of the most beautiful ships in the world. Her portrait adorned shipmasters licenses and ship registers for many years. The *Shenandoah* carried cargoes all over the world for twenty years but progress caught up with her and on June 24, 1910, she dropped anchor off Sandy Hook for the last time. Her future was to be that of a lowly barge, towed behind a steam tug. On October 29, 1915, she was rammed and sunk by the steamer *Powhatan* near Fire Island, New York with the loss of one life. A few of the coastal schooners continued to carry cargoes but could not compete with the newer ships with steam engines, fired by coal, maintaining a dependable schedule. Some of the commercial sailing vessels worked during the 1920's but, by 1930, most of them had been laid up in the backwater creeks abandoned and rotting.

In January, 1910, the Naval wireless station in Newport, Rhode Island began broadcasting the first weather information. The messages were received at the Nantucket Shoals lightship and rebroadcast on to other ships at sea. This marked the beginning of a new era in maritime safety. Radios had been installed in transatlantic liners for ship-toship or ship-to-shore communications, and weather reports. Radio communications would play a leading role in all future maritime operations.

Above: Fog and high winds were blamed for the loss of the Italian bark *Fortuna* on January 18, 1910 near Ship Bottom, New Jersey. The vessel stranded near the life saving station. The Life Savers rescued the crew of 13, the masters wife and three children by surfboat. The *Fortuna* was stripped and sold to wreckers. *Photo courtesy of Captain W.J.L. Parker, U.S.C.G.(Ret.)* Below: The schooner *J. Henry Edmunds* was anchored off Sandy Hook, New Jersey on the morning of February 2, 1910 when she was run down by a tow of barges and sunk. The crew launched their boat and rowed ashore. The schooner was a total loss. *Photo courtesy of the Mystic Seaport Museum, Mystic, Conn.*

A large passenger liner ashore presented a problem for the men of the Life Saving service but they answered the call. The 10,881 ton North German Lloyd steamer *Prinzess Irene* stranded during a thick fog on the outer bar a mile east of the Lone Hill Station on Long Island on April 6, 1911, at 4 a.m. Life Savers went aboard but the vessel was resting easy and in no danger. There were, however, 1,725 passengers on board. On the next day the Lone Hill Life Savers were assisted by others from the Blue Point and Point of Woods stations. They transferred all of the passengers to the liner *Prince Frederick* in three hours. Some of the cargo was lightered off the stranded liner and she was pulled free on April 9th and towed to New York City. *Photo by Anderson, courtesy of the Suffolk Marine Museum, West Sayville, New York.*

THE PRINZESS IRENE

One of the largest rescue efforts carried out by the U.S. Life Saving service occurred on April 6, 1911 when the 10,881 ton North German Lloyd steamer *Prinzess Irene* stranded on Long Island, New York in thick fog as she was completing a journey from Mediterranean ports to New York City with 1,725 passengers with a crew of 263 and carrying a large general cargo. There was much consternation among the passengers. Life Savers from the Lone Hill station along with others from the Blue Point station boarded the steamer to quiet the fears of the those on board. The large steamer was hard aground and Life Savers carried messages to shore to be forwarded to the vessel's owners, underwriters, revenue cutters and wreckers. Soon after, the revenue cutters Seneca and Mohawk and the wrecking steamer Relief arrived. Arrangements were made to salvage the vessel and to remove the passengers. The next day, another North German Lloyd steamer, the *Prince Frederick* arrived off shore and transfer of the passengers began at two in the afternoon. Three boats from the Life Saving stations along with five from the revenue cutters and two from the wrecking steamers brought off all 1,725 passengers without any incidents or injuries. Calm seas contributed to the prodigious undertaking. The ship was pulled off the Long Island sands three days later by removing some of her cargo and employing several wrecking steamers. Loss to the company was listed as $70,000.

Above: The Norwegian steamer *Moldegaard* underway from Baltimore to Felton, Cuba with a cargo of structural steel stranded on Cat Island in the Bahamas on November 27, 1911. Wreckers unloaded part of her cargo to try and re-float her but, she was hard aground and was declared a total loss. *Photo from the collection of Paul C. Morris, Nantucket, Mass.*
Below: On December 31, 1911, the steamer *Alpha*, bound from Philadelphia to Atlantic City, missed the inlet, broke off her rudder post and stranded on the south shoals. She was hard aground and wreckers had to remove her cargo to free her. She was pulled off on January 14 and towed to Philadelphia. Damage was listed at $6,000. *Photo from a souvenir post card.*

SS. "THISTLEROY" BR.
Ashore Lookout Shoals, N.C.
Jan. 14, 1912.

Above: The British steamer *Thistleroy*, 4,027 tons, enroute from Tampa, Florida to Liverpool with a cargo of cotton stranded on Lookout Shoals, about three miles offshore from Cape Lookout, North Carolina, on December 28, 1911. The vessel and cargo were valued at $310,000. An attempt was made to salvage the cargo by wrecking crews whose lighter is seen alongside the steamer which was a total loss. **Below:** On January 17, 1912, the British steamer *Trebia* ran aground in the same area almost ramming the other vessel. Tugs were called to the scene to refloat the vessel. On the next day the *Trebia* was pulled off and then towed to Norfolk, Virginia. She was inspected and found seaworthy and was allowed to proceed to her destination. *Photos from the Collection of Paul C. Morris, Nantucket, Ma.* The *Thistleroy* lies at approximately 34-32.4 N and 76-31.2 W

SS. "TREBIA" BR.
Ashore Lookout Shoals, N.C.
Jan. 17, 1912.

Above: On the night of April 14, 1912, the 66,000 ton White Star liner *Titanic*, on her maiden voyage to America struck an iceberg four hundred miles south of Newfoundland and foundered, taking over 1,500 people to their deaths. The *Titanic* carried lifeboats for only half of her passengers and her loss is considered the greatest maritime tragedy in the history of ocean travel. *Photo courtesy of the Titanic Historical Society,Inc., Indian Orchard, Massachusetts.* The grave of the *Titanic* was originally positioned at approximately 41-46 N, 50-14 W. **Below Left:** The women of America erected a monument to the men who went down with the *Titanic* on April 15, 1912. The memorial is in Washington Channel Park in Washington, D.C. in the southwest portion of the Nation's capital city. **Below Right** The base of the statue has an inscription which carries the thoughts of those who erected it. *Photos by the Author.*

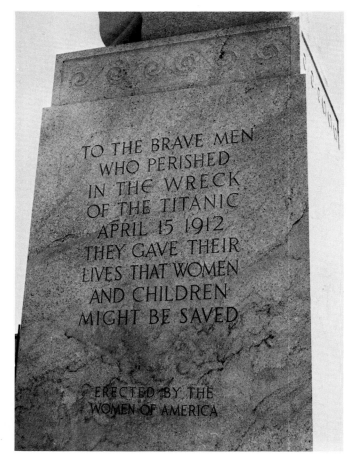

On April 14, 1912, the greatest tragedy in modern maritime history occurred when the steamer *Titanic* struck an iceberg, 400 miles southeast of Newfoundland and sank two hours later to the ocean floor, two miles below the surface. No other maritime disaster in history has so captured the headlines and continues to do so to the present day. Her story is well known; the brand new White Star liner was steaming along in the North Atlantic at 22 knots on her maiden voyage to the United States. Despite repeated warnings, just before midnight, the ship hit a huge iceberg. Her location was flashed by radio to all the ships at sea to come to her aid. The coordinates were 41-46 north and 50-14 west. The iceberg had torn a ruptured the side of the ship underwater and she was sinking. The vessel was equipped with fourteen lifeboats, two cutters and four collapsible boats with a capacity of 1,178 persons, or, a little more than half of the 2,206 persons aboard the liner. There were 1,503 persons lost. Only 706 people survived in the lifeboats. The popular illusion that the ship was unsinkable persisted in the minds of many passengers until most of the boats had left and it was too late when the terrible truth was realized. There were eleven millionaires aboard the *Titanic* along with the cream of European and American society, including John Jacob Astor. These men went down with the ship. Since the disaster, many books have been written about that memorable night. Hollywood has created movies about the *Titanic* and interested marine buffs formed a society devoted to the memory of the ship. Following the sinking the International Ice Patrol was established in the north Atlantic. The patrols continue to this day and each nation using the northern steamer routes pays its share of the expense. Every year the anniversary is marked by a Coast Guard plane dropping a ceremonial wreath near the spot where the ship went down. In September, 1985, the wreckage of the *Titanic* was located by an expedition from the Woods Hole Oceanographic Institution. The hull was found by two remote control submersibles at a depth of approximately 13,000 feet. The story of this discovery is detailed in Chapter eleven.

The schooner *James Duffield*, from Portland, Connecticut for Philadelphia with a cargo of brownstone went ashore in a storm at Cape Henlopen, Delaware early in the morning on April 30, 1912. Life savers from the Cape Henlopen station launched the surfboat and removed the crew of five and landed them ashore. The schooner and cargo were a total loss. *Photo from the collection of Paul C. Morris, Nantucket, Mass.*

Above: The dredge #4 of the Bay State Dredging Company of Boston, Massachusetts was struck by a steamer on June 25, 1912 and sunk in the St. Croix River, three miles below Calais, Maine. The salvage vessel *Commissioner* and the salvage barge Admiral were brought from New York. They raised the dredge the following September. **Below:** The British steamer *Wyvisbrook*, bound from Pensacola, Florida, to Greenock, Scotland ran aground during the night on Pebble Shoals, two miles south of the False Cape Virginia Life Saving Station on June 20, 1912. The deck load of lumber was thrown overboard. Two days later U.S. Revenue cutters pulled her off and she continued her voyage after a hull inspection. *Photos from the collection of Paul C. Morris, Nantucket, Mass.*

In 1914, the United States Congress enacted legislation to improve the government rescue teams on land and sea. On January 28, 1915, President Woodrow Wilson signed the Coast Guard Act and the merger was consummated two days later. The act combined the Revenue Cutter service and the Life Saving Service into one unit. The Revenue Cutter Service was established in 1790. The Life Saving Service was a collection of congressional acts dating from 1848. The operations were incomplete and scattered for many years. Corrective legislation was enacted but formal institution did not occur until 1878. The work of life saving along the coast was carried out by both services operating as separate organizations. Crews of the Life Saving stations and Revenue Cutters often cooperated in rescue work. These involved extensive duplication of efforts so the consolidation increased the efficiency between the shore and sea units.

The principal duties assigned to the Coast Guard were as follows:

1. Rendering assistance to vessels in distress and saving life and property.
2. Destruction or removal of wrecks, derelicts and other floating dangers to navigation.
3. Extending medical aid to United States vessels engaged in deep-sea fisheries.
4. Protection of the customs revenue.
5. Operating as part of the Navy in time of war or when the President shall direct.
6. Enforcement of law and regulations governing anchorage of vessels in navigable waters.
7. Enforcement of law relating to quarantine and neutrality.
8. Suppression of mutinies on merchant vessels.
9. Enforcement of navigation and other laws governing merchant vessels and motor boats.
10. Enforcement of law to provide for safety of life on navigable waters during regattas and marine parades.
11. Protection of game and the seal and other fisheries in Alaska, etc.
12. Enforcement of sponge-fishing law.

The Coast Guard was the "catch-all" service. Any duty not specifically designated to the Army, Navy or Marine Corps was assigned to the Coast Guard. The annual report for the fiscal year ending June 30, 1915 outlined some of the various duties falling on this service: "Warnings to vessels running into danger, medical and surgical aid to the sick and injured, recovery and burial of bodies cast up by the waters, extinguishing fires at wharves, dwellings, and business structures and fighting forest fires; cooperating with local authorities in the maintenance of public order and apprehending thieves and other lawbreakers; preventing suicide; restoring lost children to their parents; recovering stolen property and salving miscellaneous articles from danger or destruction; acting as pilots in cases of emergency; furnishing food, water, and fuel to vessels in distress; protecting wrecked property, and furnishing transportation and assistance to the branches of the public service." There were other situations to come which would test the fortitude and patience as well as add to the duty roster of the Coast Guard. The Volstead Act, or Prohibition was ratified by the necessary thirty-six states in January, 1919. Times changed abruptly for the Coast Guard. The prevention of smuggling was an old duty for the service but the rumrunners were to prove a match for the enforcement capability of the Coast Guard.

Above Left: Dense fog was the cause of a collision between the Fall River liner *Commonwealth* and the battleship *New Hampshire* on July 7, 1912, in the harbor at Newport, Rhode Island. It was early in the morning and the accident caused extensive damage to both vessels. The passenger steamer ran into the stern of the military vessel. *Photo courtesy of the U.S. Navy.* **Above Right:** One man was injured on the *New Hampshire*. There were no injuries on the *Commonwealth*. The damage laid the sound steamer up for about a month during the busy summer season. *Photo courtesy of the Steamship Historical Society of the America.* **Below:** Steamships seldom grow old and age gracefully. When they outlive their usefulness they are consigned to the breakers yards. In New York, the steamers (L. to R.) *Princeton, Newark & Naiad* lie in wait to be dismantled. *Photo courtesy of the Mystic Seaport Museum, Mystic, Conn.*

The Coast Guard as organized was a part of the military forces of the Government. The military system of the former Revenue Cutter service was utilized as a foundation for the organization of the Coast Guard. This required many changes in the status of the former Life Saving service personnel. That service had no retirement benefits for its members. The transfer of personnel of the Life Saving service to the Coast Guard was accomplished by issuing appointments as Warrant Officers and Petty Officers to the former Keepers and No. 1 Surfmen. Prior to the establishment of the Coast Guard, the Life Saving Station Keepers and No. 1 Surfmen enjoyed excellent employment status and tended to keep their jobs well into their 60's. When the Coast Guard appointments were made, a majority of these men took advantage of the new benefits and applied for immediate retirement.

The act which passed Congress and was signed by the President provided:

"That there shall be established in lieu of the existing Revenue Cutter Service and the Life Saving Service, to be composed of those two existing organizations, with the existing offices and positions and the incumbent officers and men of those two services, the Coast Guard, which shall constitute a part of the military forces of the United States and which shall operate under the Treasury Department in time of peace and operate as a part of the Navy, subject to the orders of the Secretary of the Navy, in time of war or when the President shall so direct. When subject to the Secretary of the Navy in time of war the expense of the Coast Guard shall be paid by the Navy Department: Provided, That no provision of this act shall be construed as giving any officer of either the Coast Guard or the Navy, military or other control at any time over any vessel, officer, or man of the other service except by direction of the President.

"Sec.2 * * * All duties now performed by the Revenue-Cutter Service and Life Saving Service shall continue to be performed by the Coast Guard, and all such duties, together with all duties that may hereafter be imposed upon the Coast Guard, shall be administered by the captain commandant, under the direction of the Secretary of the Treasury."

In May 1919, a Navy airplane made history when it became the first to cross the Atlantic ocean. The NC-1, NC-3 and the NC-4 flew from Long Island, New York to Trepassey, Newfoundland. From there, they crossed the Atlantic to the Azores. The NC-1 and the NC-3 ran into bad weather and had to ditch short of their goal but the NC-4 continued on and landed at Horta. Three days later, the flight continued on to Lisbon and finally to Plymouth, England. The flight, interrupted by stops for repairs and weather problems took 24 days but the mission was accomplished and the Atlantic had been crossed in an airplane. The pilot was Lt. Elmer E. Stone, of the U.S. Coast Guard. Tremendous advances in aircraft development have followed. The air arm of the Coast Guard is an important function of the "Search and Rescue" operations.

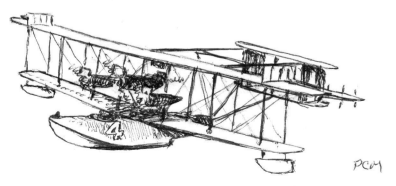

The NC-4 was the first plane to cross the Atlantic Ocean.

Above: On September 2, 1912, the Merchants & Miners steamer *Nantucket* caught fire at Locust Point in Baltimore, Maryland. Firefighters filled her upper decks with too much water and she rolled over. The Merritt, Chapman wrecking company of New York City, raised her and she went later back into service after repairs. *Photo courtesy of the Mariners Museum, Newport News, Virginia.* **Below:** Two thousand members of New York's Hudson County Democratic Club boarded the steamer *Perseus* on the evening of September 11, 1912 for an outing. The steamboat accidentally ran up on a reef opposite the College Point ferryhouse and punched a hole in her hull below the waterline. She began to sink but quick action by two passing tugboats saved the day. The tugs pushed the *Perseus* across to the ferry slip and her sister ship the *Sirius* was nearby to aid in removing the Democrats. Everyone got off safely and the vessel was later salvaged. *Photo courtesy of Mystic Seaport Museum, Mystic, Connecticut.*

Above: The barkentine *Antioch*, from Savannah for New York, stranded about 500 yards from shore near the Squan Beach L.S. Station in thick weather on March 26, 1913. The Life-savers rigged the breeches buoy but had to use a team of horses to keep the hawser taut because of the force of the current. The rescue took twelve hours to complete. Life-savers landed ten men from the grounded vessel. Keeper Longstreet of the Squan Beach station broke four hawsers in completing the rescue. *Photo courtesy of Capt. W.J.L. Parker, U.S.C.G. (Ret.)* **Below:** At about 4:30 a.m. on the morning of September 6, 1913, at Philadelphia, Pennsylvania, the steamer *Penn* caught fire in the galley and burned out of control. The steamer *Bristol*, which was alongside was badly burned on the exterior, but was pulled away from the fire by the tug *Transit*. The photograph shows the *Penn* sunk at her pier and the *Bristol* tied to the end of the pier. Damage was listed at $40,000. The *Penn* was later raised and repaired. *Photo courtesy of the Mariners Museum, Newport News, Virginia.*

Above: The four masted schooner *Marjory Brown* sank in the Atlantic on October 20, 1913 off the coast of Long Island, New York, at Lat.40-35N,Lon.71-32W. This dramatic photograph was taken by a crewman of the German passenger steamer *Berlin*, as a boat from that vessel took the crew off the sinking schooner. The boat is just astern of the *Marjory Brown*. *Photo courtesy of Paul C. Morris, Nantucket, Mass.* **Below:** There are many varied reasons why ships sink. On December 8, 1913, the *SS Zulia* was loading cargo at a pier in Brooklyn, New York when a heavy steel shaft broke through its case and fell into the hold damaging the vessel and causing a bad leak. The ship was towed to the mud flats off Red Hook, New Jersey where she sank with her decks awash. She was refloated by the Merritt Chapman Company and taken to drydock for repairs. *Photo courtesy of the Mariners Museum, Newport News, Virginia.*

Above: On October 15, 1914, in the Ambrose Channel outside New York City, a dense fog rolled in and blanketed the waterway. The United Fruit steamer *Metapan* entering port from South America was struck near the bow by the freighter *Iowan*. The Captain of the *Metapan* piloted his ship into shoal water and and rammed her into the bank to keep her from sinking. The 76 passengers and 92 crewmen were all saved. The vessel was later raised and repaired. *Photo courtesy of the Mariners Museum, Newport News, Virginia.* **Below:** The British bark *Invermay*, in ballast. came ashore early in the morning of April 12, 1915, on the beach at Mantoloking, New Jersey. The bark was driven off course by a storm and the Captain could not get his bearings. The vessel was pulled off the next day and towed to New York to take on a cargo of wheat for the British Army. *Photo courtesy of Captain W.J.L. Parker, U.S.C.G. (Ret.)*

Above: The tug *Daniel Willard* is pictured in Newport News drydock after being raised and her bow patched. In March, 1916, the steamer *Madison* rammed the tug and did considerable damage. It is interesting to note the unique method of repair on the hull. After the water drained out of the vessel, she was repaired. *Photo courtesy of Steven Lang.* **Below:** A collision at three a.m. on September 9,1916, sent the coasting schooner *Marguerite* to the bottom of Boston Harbor. The steam lighter *Eureka*, outbound, hit the schooner on her port side forward and she sank in one minute near Castle Island. The four crewmen jumped into a dory being towed astern and were picked up by the *Eureka* which was not damaged. The schooner was a total loss. *Photo courtesy of the Peabody Museum of Salem.*

Ship "Clan Galbraith".
Near Shinnecock, Long Island.
July 22, 1916.

Above: The Norwegian bark *Clan Galbraith*, in heavy weather and dense fog ran aground near Shinnecock Inlet, Long Island, New York, on July 22, 1916. The four masted steel bark was in ballast from England to the United States to take on a cargo of oil. The 2,168 ton square rigged vessel lay on the sands for about two weeks. Tugs from New York floated the ship on August 4th. She was later sunk by a German U-boat in World War II. *Photo from the collection of Paul C. Morris, Nantucket, Mass.* **Below:** The United States Transport *Sumner* bound for New York City from Colon, Panama, went aground in dense fog near Barnegat, New Jersey, on December 11, 1916. The steamer had 800 tons of scrap iron in her forward hold and she was hard on the bar. The 232 passengers went down over rope ladders into Coast Guard motor lifeboats and were brought ashore. The ship broke up on the bar and was a total loss. *Photo courtesy of the Mystic Seaport Museum, Mystic Connecticut.*

U. S. T. "SUMNER",
NEAR BARNEGAT, N. J.,
DEC. 13, 1916.

Above: Winter ice takes a heavy toll on fishing vessels. This is the *Rex*, ice bound in Boston Harbor on January 2, 1918, while her crew walked across the frozen waters. An ever present danger was the passage of a large vessel, moving the ice and crushing the small schooner. The *Rex* worked her way out of Boston harbor. She sailed until June of 1925 when she was sunk with the loss of her crew of thirteen men. She was in a collision with the British steamer *Tuscania*. **Below:** The American steamer *St. Paul* was being transferred from a drydock at the Erie Basin in Brooklyn, New York on April 25, 1918, to her berth at pier 61, North River. As she came alongside the pier she suddenly listed to port. She turned over on her side and sank in the mud. Cause of the accident which took three lives, was thought to be an ash port left open on the port side. It required five months to refloat the huge vessel. She was towed to a dry dock in Brooklyn and overhauled. *Photos courtesy of the Mariners Museum, Newport News, Virginia.*

Above: The U.S. tanker *Frederick R. Kellogg* was torpedoed and partially sunk by a German submarine on the night of August 13, 1918, thirty miles south of Ambrose Channel Lightship off Long Island, New York. Seven of her 42 man crew were reported missing. The ship was salvaged and continued to sail. *Photo courtesy of the U.S. Naval Historical Center, Washington, D.C.* **Below:** Another victim of German Uboats was the five masted schooner *Dorothy B. Barrett* on August 14, 1918 off Cape May, New Jersey. A German submarine crew placed bombs aboard the coal laden vessel and sent her to the bottom. Her crew landed at Cape May. The submarine was attacked by American sea planes and surface patrols but the results were not confirmed. It was reported to be the same U-boat that sank the *Frederick R. Kellogg* the day before. *Photo courtesy of the Mariners Museum, Newport News, Virginia.*

Above: On February 28, 1919, the liner *Aquitania* collided with the British freighter *Lord Dufferin* in New York harbor. Damage to the freighter was extensive and resulted in lengthy lawsuits. The ship lost about forty feet of her stern. The hull was immediately beached. She was refloated on March 21st. *Photo courtesy of the Mariners Museum, Newport News, Virginia.* **Below:** There are some tricky currents that plague pilots in the Cape Cod Canal. Traffic was interrupted on April 16, 1919 when the Metropolitan liner *Belfast* collided with the Sagamore draw bridge at 6 a.m. The liner hit a sheer current in the canal just before passing through the draw and demolished her forward upper works. The accident injured three people. The ship lay under the bridge through one tide and was then towed to Boston for repairs. *Photo by Small, Buzzards Bay, Mass.*

CHAPTER FIVE

The first lighthouse on the Atlantic coast was built on Little Brewster Island in Boston Harbor. It was first lighted on September 14, 1716. The first Keeper was George Worthylake. He was paid a salary of fifty pounds per year. He also served as a pilot for vessels entering the harbor. In 1776, the light was destroyed by British forces while evacuating Boston under fire. The Massachusetts Legislature voted to expend 1,450 pounds to erect a new lighthouse. That light still stands today. There are other lighthouses around Boston harbor, but there is only one Boston Light.

Congress enacted laws to create the U.S. Lighthouse Service in 1789 to "support, maintain and repair the lighthouses, fog signals, beacons and buoys on the bays, inlets and harbors of the United States for the purpose of assisting the navigation and safety of marine traffic." Heretofore the individual coastal states maintained the navigational aids and there were no standards to adhere to; consequently the upkeep was inadequate for safety. Under Government supervision there was progress however; in 1815, the U.S. owned and maintained 84 lighthouses on the coasts of eleven states. In 1872, the number had grown to 573 lighthouses and 22 lightships. Additionally there were 33 fog signals, 354 beacons and 2,762 buoys. There were 809 Light Keepers employed who were paid $350 per year for their services.

Until 1852, the Lighthouse Service was directed by an Undersecretary of the U.S. Treasury. There were many deficiencies in the service and this resulted in a sweeping reorganization which led to the creation of the Light House Board. This board consisted of the Secretary of the Treasury, officers of the U.S. Army and Navy and civilian scientists. The new board instituted improvements in the service, erected new lighthouses where needed and brought the corps from the worst lighthouse service in the world to the finest.

It was difficult to become a lighthouse keeper in the early days. A long period of apprenticeship was required and the rules were strict: "The lighthouse keeper must be over 18 years old, be able to read and write and be competent in his duties. Women and servants must not be employed in the management of lighthouses".

The new lighthouses were erected with stones, cast iron and bricks. The structures were built with various designs to blend with the local landscape and for easy identification. Many of the beautiful lighthouses built in the 19th century are historic landmarks today and continue to be subjects of artists and photographers. Several lights were situated on offshore islands aggravating maintenance of supplies, both material and sustenance. The keepers were called "Wickies" because some of their daylight hours were spent cleaning the oil burning wicks. A fresh wick would always burn clean and bright. The light had to be lit from sunset to sunrise in all weather, fair and foul. Many keepers distinguished themselves as life-savers. The *U.S.S. ALACRITY* was wrecked on ice covered ledges off Boston Light on February 3, 1918. Keeper Jennings along with his assistants rescued twenty-four sailors over the icy rocks and ledges off the island. Life at the lighthouse was never dull. Weather caused numerous problems and sometimes could exhaust the Keeper and his family. A prolonged fog, necessitating continuous fog horns could keep the soundest sleeper awake for days.

The Lighthouse service continued until July 1, 1939 when the service was consolidated with the Coast Guard. Today the Coast Guard maintains over 46,000 aids to marine navigation. Most of these are automated lights and buoys. There are 70 loran stations, 200 radio beacons and 2,200 fog signals.

ROSE HEAD

SCHR "CHARLES A. RITCE

The Nova Scotia schooner *Charles A. Ritcey* was bound from San Sebastian, Spain for Lunenburg on September 15, 1920, when she struck on Rose Head, six miles from the harbor entrance. When the vessel sank, the crew was saved but Captain Acker was lost. *Photo courtesy of a Friend.*

Above: The schooners *Charles H. Trickey* on the left and the *Mary E. Olys* both hit the ledges at the entrance to Cape Porpoise in Maine. Both Captains were trying to seek shelter from a storm and were wrecked on January 1, 1920. *Photo courtesy of Capt. W.J.L. Parker, U.S.C.G. (Ret.)* **Below:** The *Blanche C. Pendleton II* was rammed and sunk off Bodie Island, North Carolina on January 21, 1921 by the steamer *I.C. White*. The schooner was loaded with coal and the accident occurred on a clear night. There were no injuries. *Photo courtesy of the Mariners Museum, Newport News, Virginia.*

THE CARROLL A. DEERING

There are many fascinating mysteries of the sea. The puzzle of the *Marie Celeste* has never been solved and the enigma of the schooner *Carroll A. Deering* is stranger still. On a passage from Rio de Janeiro in ballast, the vessel made a stop at Barbados, British West Indies and then set sail for Norfolk, Virginia. On January 29, 1921, the schooner passed the Lookout Shoals Lightship off Cape Hatteras, North Carolina. A storm blew up after that and the next time the vessel was seen was on the 31st when she was spotted at dawn by a surfman on beach patrol. She had all sails set and was hard aground on Diamond Shoals. The seas were extremely high when the surfmen rowed out to the grounded schooner. They could not get close enough to go aboard because of the heavy swells. There were no signs of life aboard and the heavy seas were washing over the ship.

Four days later, the ocean flattened down somewhat and the surfmen went aboard the stranded vessel. At this time, the mystery deepened. In the cabin, food was on the table with a fire going in the stove. There were no signs of foul play. The ghost schooner had been abandoned by all except the cat; a mute witness. No trace of the crew or the yawl boat was ever found. No one has any knowledge of what went on during the last time the vessel was seen by the lightship and when she was found wrecked on the shoals. Was it mutiny, piracy or murder? One theory was that the ship was attacked by rum runners. Many other ideas were put forward. The crew could have been washed overboard in the storm. No distress signals were ever sent out from the schooner. No evidence has ever been found to substantiate any theory.

Investigations into the incident were held by the Navy, Coast Guard and the Treasury, State, Commerce and Navigation Departments. The official Government report in the annual list of Merchant Vessels stated that the ship was lost by stranding on Cape Hatteras with the loss of eleven men. The families of the crew suspected foul play was involved. There are many unanswered questions in the evidence that is known. Later the vessel broke up and her pieces washed ashore. Today, the skeleton of the ghost schooner lies buried in the sands of Ocracoke Island on the outer banks of Cape Hatteras, North Carolina. A grim reminder of a mystery that only the dead crew can answer.

Above: The British tramp steamer *Wandby* was lost in the fog on March 9, 1921 and piled up on the rocks at Walkers Point in Kennebunkport, Maine. The vessel lay stranded for weeks while various salvage attempts were made. She was finally cut up for scrap and was a total loss. *Photo taken in 1921 by the Whitcomb Studio, Kennebunkport, Maine.* **Below:** On September 18, 1921, about six miles south of Montauk Shoals, off Long Island, N.Y., in thick fog, the steam collier *Malden* was in a collision with the *S.S. Johancy*. The *Malden* was holed in her port side forward of the bridge. The next evening, while under tow, she sank onto a sand bar just east of Washington Shoal, near Montauk Point. With her decks awash, she was a menace to navigation and was later destroyed. *Photo by Bob Beattie, Belfast, Maine.* The wreck of the *Malden* lies at 41-05.8 N, 71-52.4 W

On December 9, 1921, the submarine S-48, while operating with a civilian crew was undergoing trials in Long Island Sound when a leak was discovered. A large amount of water seeped in. When it came in contact with the batteries, chlorine gas was formed and vessel would not surface. The crew lightened the bow compartment until it projected above water. The 40 men crawled out through a torpedo tube and clung to the hull for eight hours until a passing tug picked them up. *Photo courtesy of the Naval Historical Museum, Washington, D.C.*

THE JAMES M.W. HALL

The schooner *James M.W. Hall* left Charleston, South Carolina, for Boston on January 5, 1922 with a cargo of lumber. Soon after leaving, they met with a fierce storm and the seas tossed the small schooner around so much she developed leaks. With all hands at work on the pumps, the leaking could not be controlled. The vessel was down in the sea but her cargo kept her afloat. The crew fought for two days to save their vessel but finally had to give up. They sent up distress signals and were picked up by the steamer *West Canon* and brought into New York City. The schooner with 516,567 feet of kiln dried lumber was abandoned in latitude 39-20 N. and longitude 70-25 W. The Coast Guard Cutter *Seneca* took the vessel in tow on January 16th at 39-25 N and 70-02W and towed her to New York, arriving on January 18, 1922.

The schooner *James M.W. Hall* sailed from Charleston, South Carolina for Boston on January 5, 1922, with a cargo of 516,567 feet of kiln dried lumber. The vessel met heavy gales and rough seas. On January 10, the schooner sprung a leak and filled until her decks were awash. The crew battled to save their ship until January 15th when they were rescued by the steamer *West Cannon* underway from Gibraltar for New York. The derelict, floating on her cargo, was picked up by the Coast Guard Cutter *Seneca* and towed to New York. *Photo courtesy of the U.S. Coast Guard, Washington, D.C.*

The British steamship *Mayari*, bound from Boston for New York, grounded on the west side of Harts Island, New York, on February 21, 1923 and was high and dry. A period of low tides prevented salvagers from refloating the vessel until February 27th when she was pulled off and later arrived at her berth in New York City. *Photo courtesy of the Mystic Seaport Museum, Mystic, Connecticut.*

One of the giant six-masted coal schooners was wrecked on January 12, 1924. The *Ruth E. Merrill* grounded on L'Hommedieu Shoal in Vineyard Sound, Massachusetts. The vessel had a cargo of 5,000 tons of coal aboard. The twenty year old ship had been battling a storm and her seams worked open. The pumps jammed with coal dust and could not keep up with the flooding. The schooner was run on the shoal to prevent her sinking in deep water. The crew of thirteen men came ashore at Woods Hole in the ship's boat. The vessel was a total loss. She was one of the largest schooners in the world. *Photo courtesy of the Maine Maritime Museum, Bath, Maine.*

Above: The *Sierra Miranda*, one of the last of her type was overhauled at the Newport News Shipbuilding and Dry Dock Company and renamed the *Maria Borges*. She was destined to be a coal carrier. She was loaded with a cargo for Costa Rica and anchored in the James River on March 27, 1922. That night, the ship developed a leak and sank, with only her masts showing above water. Salvage was not economically practicable so she was cut apart underwater and her cargo salvaged. Her steel hull lies in the mud of the James River at Newport News, Virginia. *Photo courtesy of the Mariners Museum, Newport News, Virginia.* **Below:** The last square rigged whaling vessel to sail from the port of New Bedford, Massachusetts was the *Wanderer*. This voyage was short however as the bark was wrecked on the island of Cuttyhunk in a gale on April 26, 1924. The crew was saved but the ship was a total loss. *Photo courtesy of the Mystic Seaport Museum, Mystic, Connecticut.*

Above: The excursion steamer *Gratitude* was returning from an outing with 288 passengers aboard when she struck a partially sunken barge in Norfolk, Virginia, harbor and sank in shoal water about 8:30 p.m. on July 26, 1924. The collision knocked people off their feet and some were thrown into the water but everyone was saved by the numerous small craft in the area at the time. The *Gratitude* was later refloated and repaired. *Photo courtesy of the Mariners Museum, Newport News, Virginia.* **Below:** On August 26, 1924, the *Esther Adelaide*, a three masted schooner was caught in a storm off Block Island, Rhode Island and was dismasted. The vessel was towed stern first into New London harbor where she was re-rigged at the Merritt Chapman Scott wharf. There were no injuries to the crewmen nor was any of her cargo of lath lost. *Photo by Bob Beattie, Belfast, Maine.*

Above: The Rum Runner *Waldo L. Stream* ran on the shoals in Muskegat channel near Nantucket, Massachusetts, on December 26, 1924. There were 2,295 cases of Canadian whisky aboard, half of which was thrown over the side by her crew trying to refloat their vessel. They were all arrested by the Coast Guard and the remaining cargo confiscated. Somehow, the storage place was discovered by local Nantucket residents and much of it "spirited" away in the night. The Nantucket surf finished the hull of the *Waldo L. Stream. Photo courtesy of Charlie Sayle, Nantucket, Massachusetts.* **Below:** In order to remain proficient in their work the Coast Guard held drills each week for the breeches buoy and lifeboats. The men from the lifeboat station are ready to fire the Lyle gun which carries the shot line out over the drill pole. *Photo courtesy of the National Archives, Washington, D.C.*

Early on the morning of January 15, 1925, the submarine S-19 grounded on Nauset Bar in Eastham on Cape Cod, Massachusetts. The crew from the Nauset Coast Guard station in Eastham launched their surfboat and attempted to row out to the grounded U-boat. When within fifty yards of the sub, a huge wave picked up the boat and flipped it over spilling the men into the frigid Atlantic waters. The Coastguardsmen managed to hang on to the overturned boat and work their way to shore where local persons were there to help them. Other than a dunking, no one was injured. The submarine lay on the bar for three months before it was pulled off. The vessel just offshore is the Coast Guard cutter *Tampa*. *Photo courtesy of U.S. Coast Guard.*

The most tainted era in American history occurred during prohibition. President Hoover called it the "Noble Experiment". Historians refer to it as the roaring 20's. The Volstead act became law on January 16,1920 and the country dried up temporarily. No alcoholic beverages could legally be sold. There was, however, plenty of illegal whiskey and the underworld became rich dealing in liquor. In the Atlantic, just outside the three mile limit, they set up "rum row". A line of foreign vessels loaded with liquor where small fast boats could run out, load up and then run back to the coast with their contraband cargo. It soon became big business and the men engaged in it became millionaires overnight. The control of the illegal activities fell to the Coast Guard. The rum runners had fast boats to avoid patrols and the liquor ran free until the Coast Guard acquired speedier launches to compete with the "Black boats". The rum war continued with both sides trying to outdo the other. There were many deaths and wrecks along the entire Atlantic Coastline.

On December 2, 1923, at Seabright, New Jersey, the ground swell surging in from the Atlantic brought in the bodies of two men. Floating freely about them were several cases of Scotch whisky. Authorities were puzzled as to the cause of the deaths as no boat was found anywhere nearby. One body washed ashore and the Coast Guard put out a boat to investigate and found the second body three-quarters of a mile off shore. One man carried a watch that had stopped at four o'clock and officials surmised that their boat had sprung a leak and had sunk rapidly. The weather was clear and calm and the seas were light. Papers found on the dead men identified them as New Jersey residents and relatives were contacted and identities confirmed. There were many beach-combers on the beach at Seabright throughout the day but the Coast Guard kept a close watch on the cases of Scotch whisky as they floated in and prevented any from being carried away.

Above: On Friday, March 6, 1925 the 2,075 ton Danish steamer *Sierra Morena* went aground off Cape Henry, Virginia in stormy seas and thick weather. The ship lay broadside of the beach and the crew was in no danger as they waited for the salvage vessels to go to work. The Coast Guard boarded the ship but were not needed. The ship was pulled off on March 13th after a week on the sands. **Below:** The wreckage of the schooner *Irma*, bound from Boston to a southern port was cast ashore on Bodie Island, North Carolina, during gale winds and heavy seas on April 28, 1925. The crew were all saved but the hull was a total loss and went well up on the beach. *Photos courtesy of the Mariners Museum, Newport News, Virginia.*

Above: On March 10, 1926, the United States Lines steamship *America* was at Newport News, Virginia, being reconditioned when a fire broke out. The blaze apparently was caused by a blow torch of a workman. Interiors of the vessel as well as deck houses were damaged before the flames were put out. In the photograph, the stability of the ship looks secure as there is as much water flowing out of the scuppers alongside the vessel as the fire-fighters are pouring aboard. *Photo courtesy of the Mariners Museum, Newport News, Virginia.* **Below:** The Norwegian steamer *Modig* became disabled off the Virginia coast and was taken in tow on August 22, 1926 by the Coast Guard cutter *Manning.* The vessel was towed to Baltimore for repairs. *Photo courtesy of the U.S. Coast Guard, Washington, D.C.*

Above: On November 16, 1926, the Coast Guard cutter *Morrill* was being tossed about in a southerly gale in Provincetown harbor at the tip of Cape Cod when she was blown ashore with both anchors dragging. The cutter ended up on the beach high and dry, lying against a couple of beach cottages. Three days later, the cutters *Ossipee* and *Acushnet* pulled the *Morrill* off the beach and she proceeded to Boston Navy Yard for repairs. *Photo by L.M. Snow, from the John Bell Collection, Provincetown, Mass.* **Left:** A cartoon in the Boston Globe heralded the event with some good natured fun poked at the Coast Guard and their grounded cutter.

Above: The three masted schooner *W. N. Reinhardt* lost her sails and her rudder in sixty-five mile winds during a storm off the tip of Cape Cod on December 7, 1926. The ship grounded at Race Point where Coastguardsmen saved the crew of seven using the breeches buoy. The crew was badly frost bitten and were taken to the station for medical attention. The schooner was bound from Albert, N.B. to City Island, N.Y. with a cargo of lumber and lath. Part of the cargo can be seen strewn along the beach. *Photo courtesy of Allie Ryan.* **Below:** While the storm raged on for three days the main and mizzen masts came down. The Provincetown wreckers salvaged most of the cargo but the hull was a total loss. *Photo by the U.S. Coast Guard in the National Archives.*

Above: Four experimental ships of concrete were made during World War I but the idea was not practical. The *Polias* was wrecked in Penobscot Bay on Old Cilley Ledge off Port Clyde in a blizzard on the night of February 6, 1920. Eleven of her crew were lost but twenty-seven others were rescued by the Coast Guard. *Photo courtesy of the Maine Maritime Museum, Bath, Maine* **Opposite above:** Another more visible wreck lies at Cape May, New Jersey. The steamer *Atlantus* was abandoned in 1923. In 1926, it was towed to the southern tip of the Garden State to serve as a ferry slip for the new line between Cape May, New Jersey and Lewes, Delaware. She was sunk at the end of sunset boulevard *Photo from the collection of the Library of Congress, Washington, D.C.* **Opposite Below:** It was later decided to move the ferry port to another location. The hulk of the *Atlantus* still lies at the end of Cape May although she is crumbling and falling in on herself. *Photo by the Author.*

Above: On December 11, 1926, the schooner *Charles A. Dean*, enroute from Savannah to Baltimore with a cargo of cross ties, went ashore on Frying Pan Shoals near Cape Fear, North Carolina. The Captain reported that a mutiny had taken place and he held the crew at bay with a revolver. The Coast Guard removed the crew but the Captain stayed aboard. In the photograph the Oak Island crew was assisting the C.G.C. *Modoc* in passing towing hawsers. The attempt failed and the schooner was abandoned on December 29th. The vessel became a total loss. *Photo courtesy of the U.S. Coast Guard, Washington, D.C.* **Below:** On January 4, 1927, the French ship *Richelieu* loading coal pitch at Baltimore suddenly exploded and burned. The accident killed four persons working on board. The fire in the hold burned out of control until firefighters sank the ship beside the pier to extinguish the flames. Thirty-seven men were injured in the accident. The ship was a total loss. *Photo courtesy of the Mariners Museum, Newport News, Virginia.*

Above: When vessels become disabled at sea, the men in the Coast Guard cutters try to assist. The schooner *William Bisbee* was hit by a storm in the Atlantic. The ship was thirty miles east of Cape Henry, Virginia with all her sails torn and she lost her anchors. The Coast Guard cutter *Manning* arrived on scene, shot a line to the schooner and then towed her into Norfolk, Virginia, on March 7, 1927 for repairs. **Below:** The schooner *Adelaide Day* out of Georgetown, S.C. for Bridgeport, Conn., was abandoned and set on fire on November 8, 1927, off Cape Henry, Virginia. The crew was rescued by the steamer *Gulflight*. The wreck was found 225 miles southwest of the Virginia Capes by the C.G.C.*Manning* and towed into Lynnhaven Roads on November 15. The stern of the schooner was burned to the waters edge. *Photos courtesy of the Mariners Museum, Newport News, Virginia.*

Above: The Norwegian freighter *Cibao* stranded at Cape Hatteras, North Carolina, on December 4, 1927, in a northeast gale. Her crew of 24 men were rescued by the Coast Guard using a surfboat in a hair raising adventure off the beach. The men from Hatteras could not get close to the grounded steamer with their power boat. They manned a surfboat with oars and rowed to the steamer and instructed each man to leap into the water with a line around his waist. They picked up each man out of the surf. All made it to shore safely and were cared for by the men at the station. **Below:** Four Coast Guard men in the lifeboat from the Hatteras Inlet station. In addition to rescue, these boats were used for running lines to and from cutters, carrying messages from grounded vessels to shore and back and many other errands that would be presented to the Life-savers. The old cork life-jackets were heavy and bulky but were an asset if needed in an emergency. *Photos courtesy of the U.S. Coast Guard, Washington, D.C.*

The schooner *Bainbridge* sailed from Jacksonville, Florida in early February, 1929 bound for Fairhaven, Massachusetts with a cargo of long leaf yellow pine. On February 5th she was driven ashore a mile south of the Nags Head Coast Guard station, North Carolina. Eight members of her crew and the ship's cat were rescued by surfboat. Some of her cargo washed off the deck. Later when the seas subsided the rest of the cargo was brought ashore. The vessel was a total loss but the cargo was loaded on a barge and towed to Massachusetts, arriving a little later than originally planned. *Photo courtesy of the Mariners Museum, Newport News, Virginia.*

Above: A victim of the Rum War, the Navy submarine S-4, sunk by the Coast Guard cutter *Paulding* while on maneuvers off Provincetown, Massachusetts on December 17, 1927. The photo shows the S-4 after being raised and brought to the Boston Navy Yard in Charlestown for repairs. *Photo courtesy of the Standard Times, New Bedford, Massachusetts.* **Below:** During prohibition, the Coast Guard acquired several old World War I destroyers to enable them to fight the rum war on an equal footing with the bootleggers. This is the Coast Guard cutter *Paulding* in drydock in Boston, showing the damage done to the bow by the force of the collision with the submarine S-4. *Photo courtesy of the Naval Historical Museum, Washington, D.C.*

What was probably the worst disaster during the rum war occurred on December 17, 1927 off the tip of Provincetown, Massachusetts. The Coast Guard Cutter *Paulding* had completed a patrol when she was in collision with the Navy submarine *S-4* while the sub was surfacing near Herring Cove. The converted four stack destroyer hit the submarine amidships cutting down through the hull. The sub sank in 100 feet of water and her crew of 34 men all drowned. The sub was raised three months later and was used as an experimental craft in the development of new safety measures for submarines. The new technology was applied a few years later when the submarine *Squalus* sank off Portsmouth, New Hampshire on May 24, 1939 with a crew of 59 men. The rescue efforts were successful and 33 men were brought to the surface alive, utilizing a diving bell. The other 26 men drowned in the after section of the submarine.

Prohibition ended in November, 1933, when the 21st amendment was ratified and liquor was legal again. The Coast Guard had waged a vigorous battle against the rum runners. Neither side could claim victory, as the experiment of prohibition had failed during the lawless decade. The Coast Guard were outnumbered and could only carry out their duty which they did to maintain the high standards of the service.

Disasters at sea often result in new safety rules being established for ocean liners. When the *Titanic* sank in 1912, new lifeboat regulations required a seat in a lifeboat for every person on board ship. On Saturday, November 10, 1928, the 10,494 ton steamer *Vestris* departed Hoboken, New Jersey with 199 crewmen and 129 passengers. The passengers included 37 women and 13 children. The vessel had over 6,000 tons of mixed cargo aboard and it was determined later that she was badly overloaded. Late Saturday evening the ship was noticed to have a five degree list to starboard. The weather was deteriorating and the seas began to increase. Early Sunday morning, conditions became worse and the list had increased. Water was discovered in the coal bunkers and the ship had to stop because of the heavy seas. By noon, while some 250 miles off the coast of Virginia, the list had increased to eighteen degrees. The pumps could not get ahead of the water in the hold and Sunday night the cargo shifted and broke through a bulkhead. Overnight the list grew to 32 degrees and at 10 a.m. Monday, Captain William J. Carey ordered the SOS to be sent by radio.

At noon, the scene on deck was chaotic with an extreme starboard list. The crew were trying to launch lifeboats from the port side and they were smashed against the hull. They broke up soon after they were in the water, spilling women and children into the sea. Still others were launched and the ropes froze in the rusty blocks. Five boats were successfully launched from the starboard side but were not fully loaded. The *Vestris* sank at 2:15 p.m. Survivors discovered that there wasn't any food or emergency equipment on board the lifeboats. Many ships rushed to the scene but could not locate the boats. They followed the drift line and rescued 212 persons in the boats and floating in lifejackets. Of the 116 who were lost, only 29 bodies were recovered, many of these had been mutilated by sharks. All of the 13 children were lost. Investigations following the disaster resulted in newer regulations concerning cargo lading and emergency equipment aboard lifeboats. The *Vestris* sinking remains as one of the most appalling incidents in maritime history.

Above: The steamer *West Hika*, bound from Mobile, Alabama to London radioed on April 16, 1929 that her rudder had been damaged and she was unable to make port without assistance. She was 270 miles southeast of Nantucket Island at the time. To pass the tow line, a smaller line was floated to the cutter using a life-ring which was picked up with a grappling iron. **Below:** Two thirds of the rudder had been carried away. The cutter *Mohave* arrived on scene on April 18th to tow the steamer into Boston. The weather worsened and the *Mohave* needed help. The cutter *Acushnet* arrived on the 22nd and assisted to bring the *West Hika* into port. They arrived in Boston on the 24th and the steamer had to go into drydock for repairs. *Photos courtesy of the U.S. Coast Guard, Washington, D.C.*

Above: The schooner *A. Ernest Mills* was rammed and sunk on April 4, 1929 at nine o'clock in the evening about fifty miles southeast of the Virginia coast. When the destroyer *Childs* hit the *Mills,* her Captain and two crewmen were lost. The destroyer picked up six of the crew and the schooner sank. The *A. Ernest Mills* had a cargo of salt. One month later the cargo dissolved. The hull later rose to the surface and became a derelict. She came ashore on the Virginia coast. Below: There are locations at Cape Hatteras where shipwrecks have occurred frequently. On September 23, 1929, the *Carl Gerhard,* a Swedish steamer came ashore in a storm beside the wreckage of the *Paraguay* which had been wrecked on December 4, 1927 with the loss of four men. The *Carl Gerhard* was aground with the seas sweeping over her when the Cape Hatteras Coast Guardsmen fired a shot line over the ship and set up the breeches buoy. They brought in the crew of twenty-one men and one woman, in addition to some pets that were aboard. *Photos courtesy of the U.S. Coast Guard, Washington, D.C.*

Above: The steamer *City of Rockland* was of 1,696 tons, 274 feet long and had a 1,600 horse-power steam engine. She was launched in Boston in 1900 as was the epitome of elegance. She could carry 2,000 passengers as well as 600 tons of freight. But the vessel was accident prone. She suffered numerous groundings and a few collisions in her 23 year career. On the night of September 23, 1923, she was wrecked on Dix Island at the mouth of the Kennebec River in Maine. The steamer had left Bath and was on her way to Boston in dense fog. At 7:30 p.m. there was a crash as the boat struck and then slid up on the ledge. Distress signals were sounded with the ship's whistle. Before long, the Coast Guard boarded her and removed the 350 passengers as the vessel settled by the stern. The passengers were returned to Bath where they boarded a train for Boston. At low tide, the steamer made a spectacular picture as she was balanced on her keel atop the rocks. There was a huge hole in her bow. After the vessel was hauled off the ledge, she was towed to Boston. A survey of the hull showed that it was impractical to restore her to service. The *City of Rockland* was then taken to Salem, Massachusetts where she was stripped of all usable fittings and lumber. The remainder of the hull was burned on Little Misery Island. *Photo courtesy of Paul C. Morris, Nantucket, Mass.* Below: Pieces of wrecked ships wash up along the Atlantic shores from Maine to Florida. This is the bow of the Gloucester fishing vessel *Governor Fuller* which came ashore at Coskata on Nantucket Island in the early 1930's. In 1937, the windlass was taken off the wreckage and installed on the coasting schooner *Alice S. Wentworth*. *Photo courtesy of Charlie Sayle, Nantucket, Mass.*

CHAPTER SIX

It was over one hundred years after the first lighthouse was built on the Atlantic coastline before the first lightship was placed on station at Sandy Hook, off New Jersey. The number of light vessels varied as years passed, when more stable light platforms were used in place of the floating lights. In 1917, there were 53 lightship stations in the United States. The one major weakness in the lightship was the ability to maintain proper station in bad weather when the light is needed most by the mariner. Many were torn from their moorings by the heavy storms. The Diamond Shoals lightship broke her anchor chain on August 18, 1899 in a storm and was blown ashore on Cape Hatteras, North Carolina, where the men of the Creeds Hill Lifesaving Station rescued the crew with the breeches buoy. Nine men were landed and taken to the station. The vessel lay on the beach for a month before she was pulled off and towed to Baltimore for repairs.

Duty aboard a lightship was considered to be among the worst in the Lighthouse Service. It was dangerous, but above all it was lonely. The vessels were usually anchored at some of the worst locations in the ocean and seasickness was an occupational hazard. The work was not difficult and consisted of keeping the ship clean and tending the lights. This led to much leisure time and some of this was spent in personal activities like whittling or making the famous lightship baskets to relieve the monotony. Those early lightship baskets are now rare. They command high prices in antique shops and maritime auctions today.

The dangers encountered aboard a lightship were numerous and ranged from being sunk in a storm to collisions. Lightship No. 37 at Five Fathom Bank off the entrance to Delaware Bay was lost in a gale on August 23, 1893. The storm lashed the vessel for hours and just after midnight she turned over and sank. Four of her six man crew were lost. South of Nantucket Island the shoals spread out for 35 miles or more. The most remote station for a lightship is at the end of this shoal area. On January 6, 1934 the liner *Washington* sideswiped the Nantucket lightship in dense fog, while on her station. The 24,500 ton ship ripped off a boat davit, wireless aerial and a mast grating as well as a few coats of paint. That accident was the prelude of a disaster to come. On May 15, 1934, the White Star liner *Olympic* loomed out of the fog and cut the Nantucket Lightship in half. Seven men were lost and the lightship sank in less than a minute. There were only four survivors. The radio direction finder on board the *Olympic* was remarkably precise that morning when it was tuned on to the beacon from the Nantucket Lightship and it resulted in a tragedy. Another collision occurred on September 17, 1935, when the Grace liner *Santa Barbara* hit the Ambrose Lightship and smashed her bow, just outside of New York Harbor.

On December 21, 1935, the British freighter *Seven Seas Spray* ran into the Boston lightship. The collision ripped a large hole in the side of the light vessel aft of amidships down below the water line. Quick action by the crew of the lightship prevented the loss of their vessel and she was towed into the Quincy Drydock for repairs. A relief lightship was placed on the station while repairs were completed on the Boston light vessel. The U.S. Government seized the British tramp steamer for a libel of $20,000 damage to the lightship. There were many reports of barges hitting lightships, especially around Cape Cod when a long tow would pass a light vessel and make a sharp turn causing the last barge in the tow to strike the lightship.

In 1937, there were twenty-two lightships on stations along the Atlantic coastline from Portland, Maine to St. Johns, Florida. Today, none is left. The last lightship to leave her station was the Nantucket. She was replaced by a large navigational buoy. The Coast Guard held an official retirement for the ship in the summer of 1985 in Boston, Massachusetts to end over a century of duty as an aid to navigation.

Above: The Dollar liner *President Hayes* went aground off Monomoy Point near Chatham, Massachusetts in dense fog on July 10, 1931. The 10,533 ton steamer was hard up on Shovelful Shoal for two days while the cutter *Mohave* worked to free her. The liner was enroute to Boston but was not carrying any passengers on board at the time of the grounding. She was pulled off on the 13th and proceeded to Boston. *Photo courtesy of the U.S. Coast Guard, Washington, D.C.* **Below:** In Maine, the fishing schooner *Lochinvar* ran onto a submerged reef off Portland Head Lighthouse in thick fog on October 4, 1932. The crew escaped in the schooner's dories. The vessel rolled over and sank. A Maine photographer made this spectacular photograph using the light from Portland Head lighthouse to illuminate the scene. The vessel broke up in the next storm and was a total loss. *Photo from the collection of Frank E. Claes, Orland, Maine.*

Above: The proper title for this photograph might be: "Excuse Me". The schooner *Minas Prince* and the tug *Eileen Ross* were wedged in between the bridge abutments by a falling tide in Neponset near Quincy, Massachusetts on December 18, 1933. It was necessary to hire four tugboats and a wrecking locomotive of the railroad to extricate the two vessels from their positions the next day. **Below:** The schooner *Purnell T White* capsized, while under tow, eighty miles southeast of Norfolk, Virginia, on February 9, 1934. Four men were lost in heavy weather but a Coast Guard cutter rescued the other three crewmen. The schooner had a cargo of lumber and was towed into port dismasted and waterlogged. *Photos courtesy of the Mariners Museum, Newport News, Va.*

The steamer *Morro Castle* was a luxurious liner, very popular for its tropical cruises in the 1930's. The liner had its share of troubles but, overall, was a well run ship. On the night of September 8, 1934, while on a return voyage to New York, the ship caught fire and the entire upper deck areas of the vessel were burned. A Coast Guard cutter answered the SOS and picked up many survivors in the water. *Photo courtesy of the Mariners Museum, Newport News, Virginia.*

A series of collisions and fires occurred along the Atlantic coast in the early 1930's. In September 1931, the North German Lloyd liner *Europa* hit a derelict, 450 miles east of New York City while eastbound to Europe. Captain Johnsen radioed that the liner's starboard outboard propeller was disabled and her speed was reduced from 27 to 22 knots for the remainder of the voyage across the Atlantic. When the ship hit the submerged wreckage, a tremor was felt throughout the vessel. The Captain stopped the liner and lowered a boat to inspect for hull damage but found none. On September 2, 1933, the *SS President Wilson* of the Dollar Line, collided with the *SS Coldwater* of the South Atlantic Mail Line about 80 miles south of Cape Hatteras off Cape Lookout. The *Coldwater* was carrying a cargo of turpentine which immediately burst into flames engulfing both vessels and the fire leaping almost 200 feet in the air. The bow of the *President Wilson* was stove in about eight feet and the paint was burned off the forward section of the liner. The passengers and crew of the *Coldwater* were taken aboard the *President Wilson* and brought into Newport News, Virginia. The *Coldwater* sank a half hour after the collision.

Another disaster occurred on the night of September 8, 1934, when the Ward Line steamer *Morro Castle* caught fire and burned at sea off the New Jersey coast near Asbury Park. The fire started in a locker in the writing room and before crewmen could extinguish the flames it spread to other areas and soon the whole superstructure of the liner was burning out of control. The panic that followed cost many lives. There were 87 known dead, 50 were missing but 413 were rescued. The Coast Guard cutter *Tampa* attempted to tow the burned out hulk into port but rough seas caused the hawser to break and the liner came ashore in front of the Convention Hall at Asbury Park. During the investigation that followed the fire, arson was suspected as the cause. But it was difficult to prove because the evidence was inconclusive. On the Sunday following the grounding of the ship, Asbury Park officials charged a twenty-five cent admission fee for Convention Hall Pier. They collected $2,800 from a large crowd. The money was slated to go to needy relatives of those lost on the *Morro Castle*.

There were 134 casualties, either from burning to death on board, or drowning. The burned out hulk of the *Morro Castle* ended up on the New Jersey shore at Asbury Park and attracted large crowds of tourists. *Photographs courtesy of the Steamship Historical Society of America.*

Above: The three masted schooner *Nomis* stranded on Cape Hatteras, North Carolina on August 16, 1935 in gale winds and heavy seas. Coast Guard life savers landed her crew of six but the vessel broke up in the surf. **Below:** On March 26, 1936, the freighter *Willboro* was picking her way through dense fog in Long Island sound when she ran on the rocks beside Race Rock lighthouse. The accident stove some holes in the hull of the 414-foot ship and she was hard aground. Part of her cargo was removed and this enabled tugs to pull her off the rocks on the afternoon of the 27th. They brought her into New London, Connecticut to unload. Temporary repairs enabled the vessel to steam to New York for dry-docking. *Photos courtesy of the Mariners Museum, Newport News, Virginia.*

Above: The 5,399 ton freighter *Canadian Planter* was in a collision with the freighter *City of Aukland* late at night on May 3, 1936, in dense fog. The accident occurred in Nantucket Sound and the ship sank on Horseshoe Shoal. Most of the cargo was lost but the vessel was salvaged. *Photo from the collection of Paul C. Morris, Nantucket, Mass.* **Below:** The steamer *Iroquois* ran up on Bald Porcupine Island near Bar Harbor, Maine in dense fog at 3:30 a.m. on July 12, 1936. Her bow was almost up in the trees. Later in the morning, 144 passengers were taken off and sent to New York by train. The ship suffered a hole in her bow which was patched with plank and timber. She was pulled off at high tide by the U.S. Minesweeper *Owl*. She later steamed to New York for repairs. *Photo courtesy of the Steamship Historical Society of America.*

Above: In Massachusetts, during the mid-1930's, work progressed on the widening and deepening of the Cape Cod Canal by the Federal Government. A mishap occurred to one of the dredges on January 27, 1937. The *Governor Herrick* sprung a leak and sank while digging out a boulder from the bottom. The dredge was out of the channel and did not impede ship traffic. It was subsequently raised and repaired. *Photo courtesy of Army Corps of Engineers, Cape Cod Canal.* **Below:** On April 26, 1938, the steamer *Malamton* bound from Jacksonville to Boston with a cargo of lumber ran aground on the southeast point of Block Island near the lighthouse. There was extensive underwater damage to the hull but she was refloated two weeks later and towed to New York for repairs. *Photo from the collection of Paul C. Morris, Nantucket, Mass.*

Above: The *City of Salisbury*, the noted "Zoo Ship", was entering Boston Harbor in dense fog on April 22, 1938, when she ran up on an uncharted rock near Graves Ledge. The ship was inbound from Calcutta, India and had a cargo of exotic wild animals aboard. Monkeys, trumpet birds, pythons and several deadly cobras were among the cargo. The animals were removed and the ship later broke in half and sank. The uncharted rock was charted and named "Salisbury Rock". *Photo courtesy of the Peabody Museum of Salem, Mass.* The *City of Salisbury* lies at approximately 42-22.4 N, 70-51.6 W. **Below:** About 6 p.m., on May 28, 1938, the steamer *Mandalay* was entering the narrows between Coney Island and Staten Island in New York. The fog was so thick that visibility was down to zero. The *SS Acadia* was outbound for Bermuda when she sliced into the smaller ship. The Captain of the *Mandalay* shouted to the Captain of the *Acadia* requesting him to hold his bow in the hole, which he did while the passengers made their way to the larger ship over makeshift ladders and gangways. Fifteen minutes later the *Mandalay* sank to the bottom of the bay. No one was lost but the excursion steamer was a total wreck. *Photo courtesy of the U.S. Coast Guard, Washington, D.C.*

HURRICANE!!! Those on land and at sea in the path must prepare for the onslaught of wind and wave. These storms are classed as tropical cyclones which develop where the sea surface temperature exceeds 76 degrees F. The characteristic track of a hurricane begins a little north of the equator in the Atlantic somewhere west of Africa. The storm travels west-north-west towards the Caribbean Sea. The gale begins to grow in strength and intensity as it approaches the Greater Antilles. Whirling bands of rain-filled clouds form a huge circle as the winds increase to 100 miles per hour or better. Most hurricanes are estimated to be between 100 and 300 miles in diameter with an extreme low pressure in the center, or eye of the storm.

The track begins to bend more northerly as it approaches the land masses and veers erratically. Some storms take the westerly track and pass by Cuba into the Gulf of Mexico while others turn north threatening the eastern seaboard of the U.S. This track varies and sometimes the storm heads towards land. The entire east coast from the Gulf of Mexico northward to the Maritimes is vulnerable to these killer storms.

The outer banks of North Carolina often lie in the path of these storms as they meander erratically up the Atlantic Coast. When the hurricane smashes into the low lying dunes, the angry waters move the sands and lift a curtain from the shipwreck bones of yesterday. The storms sometimes pass over Ocracoke through Cape Hatteras and northward to Nags Head and thence out to sea northward to New England. When the storm abates, the bared skeletons of shipwrecks once again remind us of the frail ships and the gales, like the hurricane of August 17, 1899 with winds of one hundred miles per hour. In this storm, the Barkentine *Priscilla* was dashed ashore and broken into pieces, three miles south of the Gull Shoal Life Saving Station. Four persons died in the wreck, ten survived. The remains of the *Priscilla* lie just under the sands until storm roiled waters reveal them, only to be covered again by the ever moving tides. Near the beach, just south of the Oregon Inlet lies the boiler and part of the smokestack of the steamer *Oriental* which sank there in 1862. Another example of the moving sands near Cape Hatteras Lighthouse is the three masted schooner *Altoona*. Wrecked in 1878, the ship was covered until the hull washed out in 1962. At Bodie Island near Coquina Beach lies the bottom section of the hull of the *Laura A. Barnes*, a four masted schooner wrecked on June 1, 1921. Off shore lie the sunken hulls of hundreds of ships. Deep on Diamond Shoals lies the Civil War ironclad *Monitor*, which sank in a storm in 1862 while under the tow of the steamer *Rhode Island*. Sixteen of her crew went to the bottom with her. The wreck is in 220 feet of water about sixteen miles southeast of Cape Hatteras and has been declared a marine sanctuary. This status is similar to that of a National Park or monument. The *Monitor* lies in gallant company, joined by hundreds of merchant seamen during the second World War when the German U-boats littered the bottom with torpedoed merchant ships.

One of the most devastating storms to hit the eastern seaboard of the United States was the killer hurricane and tidal wave of September 21, 1938. The state of Rhode Island was inundated with tidal waters almost fourteen feet above mean high water. There were 600 deaths and over three hundred million dollars in property damage. Entire communities were wiped out. All of the waterfront areas of the state, along with ships, boats, docks and piers were destroyed. Communications were severed completely. It was weeks before normal services could be restored.

On April 22, 1938, the steamer *City of Salisbury* was entering Boston harbor in a dense fog when she was impaled on an "uncharted rock" on Graves Ledge. The ship was inbound from Calcutta, India and had a cargo of exotic wild animals aboard. Among the creatures were monkeys, trumpet birds, pythons and several deadly cobras. The ship was hard aground, and the wave action was grinding away at the hull. Ominous groans of the tearing steel plates echoed throughout the hull as the swells tipped the ship back and forth like a pendulum. The animals were removed but a portion of the rest of the cargo was lost. The ship broke in half and disappeared a few months later.

Above: On September 21, 1938, a hurricane smashed into southern New England along the Rhode Island coastline and did over three hundred million dollars in damage. The tanker *Phoenix*, laden with 57,000 gallons of gasoline, dragging both anchors was tossed up on the shore at Somerset, Massachusetts. **Below:** The summer excursion steamer *Monhegan* was sunk at her pier in Providence, Rhode Island. *Photos by R. Loren Graham, courtesy of the Steamship Historical Society of America, Inc.*

Above: The Newport-Jamestown ferry *Governor Carr* was driven ashore at Jamestown by the high winds and waves. *Photo courtesy of the Mariners Museum, Newport News, Virginia.* **Below:** A new high for tidal waters in Providence was reached by the storm as it measured thirteen feet, eight and a half inches above mean high water. Sue Ewen stands beside the brass plaques on the wall of the historic Old Market House in Market Square. *Photo by Bill Ewen.*

The Texaco tanker *Lightburne* ran aground on February 10, 1939, in dense fog on the southeast end of Block Island with 72,000 barrels of gasoline and kerosene aboard. The grounding caused some hull damage and the vessel sank by the stern. Salvage operations were started and part of the oil removed but winter storms halted the work. The tanker broke up and was a total loss. *Photos courtesy of Paul C. Morris, Nantucket Mass.* The tanker *Lightburne* lies at approximately 41-04.3 N, 71-32.3 W

Above: On February 25, 1939, the steamer *Lillian*, was underway from Puerto Rico for New York, with a cargo of raw sugar, when she was rammed by the North German Lloyd freighter *Wiegand*. The accident occurred in dense fog about ten miles east of Barnegat lightship off the New Jersey coast. Thirty-two crewmen from the *Lillian* were taken aboard the *Wiegand* and brought to New York. The *Lillian* sank the next day in deep water. *Photo courtesy of Paul C. Morris, Nantucket, Mass.* The *Lillian* lies at approximately 40-01.5 N, 73-31.7 W **Below:** In the late 1930's most of the old schooners were rotting in the backwater ports while the steam driven ships carried most of the maritime commerce along the Atlantic coastline. One of the old four masters, the *Snetind* lay outside Boston, aground near Spectacle Island, waterlogged and decaying. There was however, life aboard. Mrs Anne Windsor Sherwin and her son William had residence aboard the old vessel and were squatters. Harbor police tried to persuade the mother and son to abandon the old hulk but they refused. The city health commissioner examined the case and reported that the mode of living adopted by the two persons was not injurious to public health so the pair continued to live aboard a few months more until they were forced to leave because of ill health. The schooner was later towed out in Massachusetts Bay and sunk. *Photo from the Authors collection.*

Above: On September 17, 1939, at 3 a.m. the 3,200 ton Norwegian freighter *Rio Branco* ran up on the rock ledges of Eastern Point at Gloucester, Cape Ann, Massachusetts. The helmsman made an error in navigation when he mistook the Eastern Point lighthouse for Boston Light, a twenty mile error. The ship was wedged on the rocks for seven days while salvagers unloaded her cargo to lighten her. She was pulled off and then proceeded to Boston for dry-docking to repair the damaged hull. *Photo courtesy of the Peabody Museum of Salem.* **Below:** Another peculiar accident occurred when the tug *Cayuga* was rolled over and sank at the mouth of the Connecticut River in Old Saybrook. The *Cayuga* and the *Celtic* were towing a barge down the river with the *Celtic* leading. When they arrived at the river's mouth, a strong tide caused the barge to veer around and the *Cayuga* was pulled over. There was no loss of life and the tug was later re-floated. The accident occurred in November, 1939. *Photo from the collection of Steven Lang.*

Above: On May 24, 1939, just after eight in the morning, the United States Navy submarine *Squalus* was on a routine training dive off the Isle of Shoals, New Hampshire, when a high speed induction valve stuck open, flooding the aft compartments. The sub sank in 240 feet of water with fifty-nine men aboard. Thirty-three of the crew were in the forward section. Shortly afterward, communications were achieved between the sunken vessel and another submarine on the surface. The Navy rushed the submarine tender *Falcon* to the scene with divers and a rescue bell. *Photo courtesy of the Portland Press Herald, Portland, Maine.* **Below:** Aboard the *Falcon*, rescue work began. A diver was lifted over the side to dive on the sunken submarine. On the left, the diving bell. *Photo courtesy of the National Archives, Washington, D.C.*

Above: Using the diving bell, they succeeded in bringing the surviving thirty-three crewmen to the surface the next day. The other 26 men in the aft section were all lost when the sub sank. **Below:** On September 14, the hull was raised and towed to Portsmouth, New Hampshire. She was repaired and went to sea again. *Photos courtesy of the Portland, Press Herald, Portland, Maine.*

Above: The United States liner *Manhattan,* bound from New York to San Francisco with 192 passengers, went aground on January 12, 1941, near West Palm Beach, Florida. The 24,289 gross ton vessel lay on a sand bar for twenty-two days and her cruise had to be canceled. The Coast Guard cutter *Vigilant* took off the passengers and ferried them to Palm Beach. After she was pulled off the bar, the ship was towed to New york for repairs. She became a troop carrier soon after and was renamed *Wakefield.* After the war, she was laid up and then sold for scrap in 1964. *Photo courtesy of the U.S. Coast Guard.*
Below: Along the Atlantic coastline there are grim reminders of shipwrecks. On Cape Hatteras, North Carolina, two broken lifeboats and some other pieces of a wooden ship washed ashore and lay on the sands of the Outer Banks. The nameless remains of another maritime loss. *Photo courtesy of the Cape Hatteras National Seashore.*

CHAPTER SEVEN

In December 1941, the Empire of Japan attacked the United States Naval Base at Pearl Harbor in Hawaii and embroiled the U.S. in World War II. America declared war on the Axis powers and began to arm the nation for the struggle ahead. The wrecks which occurred off the Atlantic shores took on a somber note as hundreds of American sailors died when their ships were torpedoed by German submarines. There were shortages of ships and crews but the American spirit and technology seemed to be able to rise to the task. An aircraft developed by the Sikorsky Company in Bridgeport Connecticut was being studied with great interest. The helicopter was tested and had proved its potential. The Navy had originally intended to use the rotary wing aircraft in anti-submarine warfare but the machine proved to be the ultimate search and rescue craft for the Coast Guard.

The shipwrecks continued throughout the war but to maintain security, photographs of disasters all but disappeared from the newspapers and the other media. On February 9, 1942, at pier 88 in New York City, a fire broke out aboard the French liner *Normandie*. She was the grandest ship afloat with luxurious accommodations and excellent cuisine for the Atlantic traveler. She was of 83,000 gross tons and her speed was rated at 31 knots. New York's fire boats pumped over 800,000 gallons of water aboard to put out the fire. However, the weight of the water caused the ship to roll over on her port side and sink in the mud. The ship was later raised but repairs proved to be too costly in time of war and she was scrapped.

Two other huge ocean liners were converted into troop ships, and after the United States entered the war, the *Queen Elizabeth* and the *Queen Mary* were used to ferry soldiers across to Europe. The carrying capacity of the Queens was larger than any of the smaller U.S. vessels. The only problem was that when the *Queen Mary* was fully laden with 16,000 soldiers, her draft increased to 44 feet 6 inches. This meant that any slight list to port or starboard and she would hit the tunnel under the Hudson River. The ship passed over the tunnel at high tide while 16,000 soldiers were distributed evenly throughout the ship with orders not to move. The formula worked and the *Queen Elizabeth* followed soon after with another division of troops. During the war, the two ships depended on secrecy and speed to evade the Nazi Uboats.

The German U-boats began a slaughter along the Atlantic coast in 1942. The toll on merchant shipping was heavy especially along the shores of North Carolina. Strict censorship at the time revealed little but the residents along the outer banks referred to the off shore area as Torpedo Junction, for as many as three or four ships at a time could be seen burning after being attacked by the U-boats. The U.S. was not prepared for the submarine warfare and the sinkings continued without abeyance. Hundreds of merchant seamen lost their lives in the unrelenting, one sided battle. One U-boat even sank the Diamond Shoals lightship. After a few months, Navy and Coast Guard ships and planes turned the tide of battle, and sinkings along the coast declined. abeyance

During the war, coast watchers kept a close lookout for submarines. Towers along the coast were manned during the daylight hours to guard against attacks. The *Oakey L. Alexander* was a small collier with low freeboard and a small superstructure. On a passage between Portland, Maine and ports to the south the ship was sometimes mistaken for a submarine. When the vessel was eight to ten miles off shore, only her upper works would show above the horizon. The resemblance to the silhouette of a submarine was remarkable. Whenever the coast watch outposts would report sighting a submarine, officials would check the location of the *Oakey L. Alexander* to avoid false alarms.

Above: The steamer *Essex*, bound from Lisbon to New York ran aground on September 25, 1941, at Block Island, Rhode Island. The steamship stranded at very near the same location as the tanker *Lightburne* in 1939 (page 109). The hull of the *Lightburne* is visible on the left side of the photograph above the rocks. The *Essex* had 39 tons of general cargo and 600 tons of cork. The accident damaged the hull and she sank. **Below:** A December storm swept the superstructure off the hull and she went to pieces soon after. *Photos courtesy of the Mariners Museum, Newport News, Virginia.*

The motor vessel *Oregon*, steaming without lights while observing wartime blackout rules, was in collision with the *U.S.S. New Mexico*. The accident occurred fifteen miles northeast of the Nantucket Lightship off the coast of Massachusetts on December 10. 1941. The freighter was struck in the bow and was down considerably when this photograph was made from a Coast Guard plane by cameraman R.J. O'Leary. The ship sank as a result of the collision and seventeen men were lost. *Photo courtesy of the U.S. Coast Guard.*

Another hurricane hit the east coast on September 14, 1944. The path of the storm went over southeastern Massachusetts and Cape Cod causing a hundred million dollars in property damage. Because of adequate warnings by the weather bureau, only 31 deaths were reported. Twelve of these occurred when the Vineyard Lightship was lost with all hands off Cuttyhunk Island. Thousands of homes were damaged, mostly by trees which were blown down in the gale winds. Summer cottages along the shoreline were broken up like kindling wood by the force of the storm. Damage was heaviest along the waterfront areas.

World War II ended in August 1945 but the maritime accidents continued. A freak collision occurred on February 24, 1946, when the 10,000 ton *Nicaragua Victory* hit the Cooper River bridge in Charleston, South Carolina. The vessel was at anchor when a sudden squall came up with high winds and forced the vessel to drag her anchors. She hit the bridge with such force that a complete section crashed down on top of the ship. An automobile carrying five persons fell off the bridge into the river killing everyone inside. Repairs to the bridge took six months to complete.

On March 3, 1947, the *Oakey L. Alexander* was battling gale winds off Cape Elizabeth, Maine when a 150 foot section of her bow was completely sheared off by the force of the sea. The ship was carrying 8,200 tons of coal bound from Norfolk, Virginia to Portland, Maine when the accident occurred. Fortunately, no one was on the bow section when it broke off but there were 32 men back aft. Captain Raymond Lewis decided to run her ashore on the ledges at Cape Elizabeth where the crew could be rescued from the beach. The Coast Guard had been monitoring the ship's progress and when she hit the rocks, they were ready. The entire crew, one by one, were landed by the breeches buoy safely. The collier was a total loss.

The war created a shortage in ships for the United States. Later, this country took over the French liner *Normandie* for conversion into a troop ship. She was built in 1935 and was the pride of the French line. She was considered the grandest liner afloat with luxury in her first class accommodations fit for kings and queens. The vessel was of 83,000 gross tons and could speed across the Atlantic at 31 knots. On February 9, 1942, during the conversion, a workman's torch ignited a pile of kapok lifejackets and the fire quickly spread to other parts of the superstructure. New York fireboats pumped over 800,000 gallons of water aboard to fight the blaze and the ship took a ten degree list to port. As workers tried to pump out water from the upper decks, the list increased to seventeen degrees. Late at night the list increased to thirty-five degrees. *Photo courtesy of the Mariners Museum, Newport News, Virginia.*

Above: The *Normandie* rolled over on her port side and lay in the mud of New York harbor. The salvage of the liner proved too costly. She was later refloated and towed to the scrap yards. **Below:** The *Anna R. Heidritter*, while anchored south of Ocracoke Island, North Carolina, was hit by a heavy southeast gale which broke her anchor gear. She went ashore on the outer bar with the seas making over her. The crew climbed into the rigging. They hung there until the next afternoon when life savers fired a shot line over her and brought them ashore by breeches buoy. The schooner was loaded with dyewood. She came ashore on March 2, 1942 and was a total loss. Her captain was Bennett D. Coleman of Springfield, Massachusetts. He cleared up his business after the loss of his ship and headed home. After surviving the shipwreck and the rescue by breeches buoy, Captain Coleman was killed in a taxicab accident in New York City while changing trains. *Photos courtesy of the Mariners Museum, Newport News, Virginia.*

Above: The war exacted a heavy toll in merchant ships off the east coast during the early months of 1942. An unidentified ship is shown after taking a torpedo amidships. She is awash and sinking. The loss in ships and men was heavy until the Navy stopped the carnage along the Atlantic shoreline. **Below:** Clinging to a liferaft tossing on stormy seas, sixteen survivors of a U.S. troop transport sunk by a Nazi U-boat were rescued by the U.S. Coast Guard Combat Cutter *Bibb*. The transport *Henry R. Mallory* was torpedoed with the loss of more than 300 American soldiers, sailors and Marines. *Photos courtesy of the U.S. Coast Guard.*

Above: On March 16, 1942 the Texas Company tanker *Australia* was torpedoed by a German submarine at 35-07 N. and 75-22 W. about twenty five miles east of Cape Hatteras, North Carolina. The explosion occurred in the engine room of the tanker killing the four crewmen on duty. The vessel then sank by the stern. There were 36 surviving crewmen who were rescued by the *SS William J. Salman* and transferred to a Navy vessel. The *Salman* was torpedoed two days later and sunk. The *Australia* was a total loss. *Photo courtesy of the Mariners Museum, Newport News, Virginia.* **Below:** On March 27, 1942, the fully loaded Standard Oil tanker *S.S. Dixie Arrow* was torpedoed by a German U-boat and sank in a smoking inferno off Cape Hatteras, North Carolina at 3454 N. and 75-45 W. A Coast Guard pilot from the Elizabeth City air station was patrolling the area and guided a destroyer to the scene. Disaster struck so quickly, the crew had only time to dive over the side. Without boats or rafts, they struggled to evade the flaming oil spreading over the water. Out of four lifeboats, only one was found later with eight survivors on board. The other lifeboats dropped empty, into the burning oil on the water. Empty life rafts floated about. Many of the crew were picked up by the destroyer. Eleven men from a crew of thirty-three were lost in the sinking. *Photo courtesy of the U.S. Coast Guard*

Above: The Socony-Vacuum Oil Company tanker *S.S. Tiger* was torpedoed on April 1, 1942, by the German submarine U-754 just outside Cape Henry, Virginia, while waiting for a pilot to con the ship to Norfolk. One crew member was killed in the attack but the other 35 crewmen and a six member Navy gun crew were saved. The tug *Relief* attempted to tow the ship into port but she sank and had to be abandoned. *Photo courtesy of the Mariners Museum, Newport News, Virginia.*
Below: At the southern end of the Cape Hatteras National Seashore lies Ocracoke Island. In Ocracoke village, there is a small cemetery which holds the remains of four British sailors. These men were washed ashore on May 14, 1942. Their ship, the *H.M.S. Bedfordshire* was torpedoed by a German submarine. There were no survivors. Two of the sailors were unidentified. The other two were Lt. Thomas Cunningham and Stanley R. Craig. *Photo by the Author.*

Above: In the spring months of 1942, the war on German submarines grew hotter. A Navy PBY dropped a bomb during anti-submarine warfare along the Atlantic coast. *Photo courtesy of the National Archives, Washington, D.C.* **Below:** On April 11, 1942, the *SS Henry F. Sinclair, Jr.* was torpedoed by the German submarine U-203, seven miles south of Cape Lookout, North Carolina at 34-25 N. and 76-30 W. The tanker was bound from Houston, Texas to Norfolk, Virginia with 68,000 barrels of gasoline and fuel oil. Out of a crew of 36 men, ten were killed. *Photo courtesy of the Mariners Museum, Newport News, Virginia.*

Above: The *Byron D. Benson* was a 7,953 ton tanker of the Tidewater Oil Company of New York. She was sailing from Port Arthur, Texas to Bayonne, New Jersey, with 100,000 barrels of crude oil when she was torpedoed by the German submarine U-552 on April 15, 1942, at 36-08 N. and 73-32 W. From her crew of 37, ten were lost in the fire. The remaining crewmen were saved by other vessels in the area. *Photo courtesy of the Mariners Museum, Newport News, Virginia.* **Below:** The German submarines exacted a heavy toll on American shipping in the North Atlantic during World War II. On April 16, 1942, a Nazi sub operating in the waters off Cape Hatteras sank the British Merchant ship *Empire Thrush.* A Coast Guard patrol plane made this photograph as the ship went under. *Photo courtesy of the U.S. Coast Guard.*

Above: The Standard Oil Company tanker *SS F.W. Abrams* while enroute from Aruba, N.W.I. to New York City carrying 90,000 barrels of fuel oil, hit an American mine off Cape Hatteras on June 11, 1942 and sank. The master was unaware of the mine field and ran right through it. The ship foundered at 34-57 N. and 75-56 W. All of her crew of 36 men were saved. *Photo courtesy of the Mariners Museum, Newport News, Virginia.* **Below:** The 7,117 ton American collier, *S.S. Santore* struck a German mine off Chesapeake Bay on June 17, 1942. She rolled over and sank. Three crewmen were lost but 35 were saved along with eight members of the armed guard aboard the vessel. *Photo courtesy of the National Archives, Washington, D.C.*

125

Above: The tanker *Pennsylvania Sun* was torpedoed on July 15, 1942 and in a short time was burning out of control. The captain ordered the crew to abandon ship and all 57 men were picked up by a U.S. Navy destroyer. They were landed at Key West, Florida. The next day, part of the crew returned to the flaming tanker with fire fighting equipment and the fire was extinguished. The tanker was towed into port where repairs were made. **Below:** The *SS Chapultepec* had better luck with a torpedo than her sister ships off Cape Hatteras. On December 26, 1943 the German Submarine U-530 attacked the tanker and the torpedo struck the bow of the ship. The vessel continued and came into Cristobal and unloaded her cargo. She then went to Galveston, Texas where she was repaired and returned to service. There were no injuries to any members of the crew. *Photos courtesy of the Mariners Museum, Newport News, Virginia.*

Above: The United States Navy began to fight the U-boat menace and started winning the war on our side of the Atlantic. The above photograph taken on June 12, 1943 shows a German U-boat under depth charge and strafing attack by aircraft from the *U.S.S. Bogue, CVE-9*. **Below:** Aboard the destroyer *U.S.S. Greer, DD-145*, a "Y" gun is fired with a depth charge during a North Atlantic convoy in June, 1943. *Photos courtesy of the National Archives, Washington, D.C.*

In late October, 1943 the 7,821 ton freighter *F. J. Luckenbach* was driven ashore in a storm at Belmar, New Jersey. The Coast Guard rigged the breeches buoy to save the crew. In the photo above, crewman William Barrett is shown coming ashore from the grounded freighter. Damage from the storm along the New Jersey shore was estimated at over one million dollars. *Photo courtesy of the U.S. Coast Guard.*

Above: There were bad times on the Atlantic when our ships hit mines or were torpedoed. This is a photograph of the *DE # 143* on August 2, 1944, after an explosion split her in half. The stern half of the ship was upright but the forward section was over on her port side and sinking. The casualty occurred on August 2, 1944 in the Atlantic. **Below:** During convoy duty in the North Atlantic our ships were on constant alert for the U-boats. This photograph was taken of the *DE-51* in a drydock on May 6, 1944 after she had rammed a U-boat. The collision bent the bow at an extreme angle. *Photographs courtesy of the National Archives, Washington, D.C.*

Above: The beginning of the end for another German U-boat. The shelling attack totally knocked out the conning tower and soon after the photo was made the sub sank. **Below:** On June 4, 1944, the Navy escort carrier's planes captured a German sub in mid Atlantic. *Photos courtesy of the National Archives, Washington, D.C.*

With the stars and stripes proudly flying above the German swastika, an American Naval officer cons the captured submarine back to port escorted by American Naval craft. *Photo courtesy of the National Archives, Washington, D.C.*

Above: On April 22, 1943, the three masted Canadian schooner *Frances Parsons* sank in an Atlantic gale and her crew survived in a lifeboat. Three days later they were rescued by a Coast Guard patrol plane. They were then transferred to a Coast Guard cutter and later landed at Norfolk, Virginia. The survivors were: Captain John Simon Smith, 80, of Lower LaHave, N.S.; Charles Nelson Conrad, 33, Mate, of Riverport, N.S.; Gordon Pringle, 23, Steward, of Toronto, Ont.; and Seamen Basil Robinson, 48, of Yarmouth, N.S.; Lloyd J.E. Whynacht, 18, of Stonehurst, N.S. and Anthony Baynes, 21, of Guadaloupe, F.W.I. *Photo courtesy of the U.S. Coast Guard.* **Below:** On February 11, 1944, the British steamship *Empire Knight*, 7,244 tons, on her way from St. John, N.B., to New York City, missed a buoy off the coast of Maine and ran up on Boon Island Ledge. A northeast storm was blowing a gale and the bow of the freighter was hard up on the ledge while the stern was tossed around by the high seas. An SOS was radioed. Coast Guard and Navy units were diverted to the area. On the scene, however, rescue was next to impossible because of the heavy storm seas. The next morning, the ship broke in half and the stern section sank almost immediately. Men and boats were tossed into the sea. The final count was 20 saved, 24 lost. Eventually the bow was smashed by the seas and sank. *Photo by the United States Navy, courtesy of the National Archives, Washington, D.C.*

Above: The New York Herald Tribune published a shipwreck photograph on October 28, 1943 of the Liberty ship *James Longstreet* ashore at Sandy Hook, New Jersey. The hull of the ship was damaged and she was high and almost dry. At low tide there was only ten feet of water between the vessel and the beach. The crew was removed by the Coast Guard and the ship lay on the sand for a month before being refloated. The *Longstreet* was towed to New York City where a survey found her to be almost a total loss. Later she was used for various purposes by the Navy but was finally towed to Massachusetts in April of 1945 and grounded on a sand bar in Cape Cod Bay. The final determination of the ship was to serve as a target for the New England military air forces, Army, Navy, Air Force and the Air National Guard. **Below:** This aerial view was made in 1978 of the *James Longstreet* as she lay in Cape Cod Bay. The accuracy of the military pilots is attested to in that the midships area is well blown out. *Photo by the Author.*

Above: While bound for Baltimore from Liverpool, the liberty ship *John Gibbon* was blown ashore at Lynnhaven roads, Virginia on December 4, 1945. The 7,200 ton ship was hard aground as the storm continued to lash her. She was later refloated. *Photo courtesy of the Mariners Museum, Newport News, Virginia.* **Below:** The operation of the breeches buoy along the Atlantic shores has been discontinued by the Coast Guard. Helicopters now rescue mariners from grounded ships but this view taken on the outer banks of North Carolina gives a good idea of the personnel required to operate the apparatus. Conversely, three men using a helicopter, can carry out the same rescue today and not get their feet wet. *Photo courtesy of the Cape Hatteras National Seashore, North Carolina.*

The freighter *Charles S. Haight* ran aground on a ledge near Rockport, Massachusetts just after midnight on April 2, 1946 during a snow storm. Three days later, the stern section broke away from the hull. The ship was stripped and was a total loss. *Photos courtesy of Paul Sherman, NORLANTIC, Hudson, New Hampshire.*

Above: On March 3, 1947, the 5,284 ton collier *Oakey L. Alexander* with 8,200 tons of coal was battling gale winds with snow and high seas outside Portland, Maine. The seas split her apart and she lost 150 feet of her bow section. Fortunately the 32 man crew were all stationed in the after section of the vessel. Captain Raymond Lewis managed to beach the crippled ship on the rocky ledges of Cape Elizabeth. *Photo courtesy of the U.S. Coast Guard.* **Below:** The Coast Guard fired a shot line to the broken collier and set up the breeches buoy. The 32 men aboard were all brought to shore safely. *Photo by Gardner Roberts, Portland Press Herald, Portland, Maine.*

After the war there were twelve German U-boats in the custody of the United States Government. One of these was deeded to the Museum of Science and Industry in Chicago and is on display there. Three were sold for scrap metal and the remainder were sunk testing torpedoes. This is the U-234, sunk on November 20, 1947 forty miles northeast of Cape Cod. She went down in 600 feet of water after being torpedoed by the U.S.S. Greenfish. *Photo from the National Archives, Washington, D.C.*

Above: The *Deliverance*, a 200 ton schooner ran aground near Ponte Vedra Beach in Florida on December 13, 1947 in the early morning hours. The vessel was enroute to Jacksonville for a load of lumber. Her crew of nine were uninjured but were taken to the Coast Guard station at Mayport for treatment of shock and exposure. *Photo courtesy of the U.S. Coast Guard.*
Below: A spectacular fire and rescue on July 3, 1948 ten miles off the coast of Delaware, as the Swedish ship *Dagmar Salen* caught fire in the engine room and burned for hours. *Photo courtesy of the Mariners Museum, Newport News, Virginia.*

The blaze on the *Dagmar Salen* continued all day and was finally brought under control early in the evening by units of the Coast Guard. Forty-two people including two children abandoned the burning ship into life boats and were picked up by another freighter nearby. One man was badly burned in the accident and the Coast Guard sent an aircraft from Floyd Bennett Field in New York to pick up John Weller, 17, who was in the engine room when the fire started. The injured man was flown to Baltimore, Maryland where an ambulance transferred him to a hospital. The vessel was towed to Newport News for repairs. *Photo courtesy of the Mariners Museum, Newport News, Virginia.*

Above: The *Joseph V. Connolly*, burned out and adrift in the North Atlantic on January 12, 1948, after a fire of undetermined origin sent the crew over the side into life boats during gale winds and freezing temperatures. Two other ships rescued the crew of 46 from the boats after they spent nine hours on the high seas. Tugs were sent to tow the hulk to port but the weather deteriorated. When the towlines parted she turned over and sank. *Photo courtesy of U.S. Coast Guard.* **Below:** An Atlantic hurricane moved up the coast in mid-September in 1948 and left a path of wreckage in its wake. The *SS Leicester* was disabled and abandoned by her crew after six of them were washed overboard during the storm. There were 39 survivors of the wrecked vessel brought ashore by rescue ships. The hulk of the *Leicester* became in salvage terms, a rich prize, and under maritime law could be claimed by the first man to put a line aboard her. This was accomplished by the crew of the *Foundation Josephine,* a Canadian seagoing tug and salvage company. The ship was later towed to Bermuda. *Photo courtesy of the Mariners Museum, Newport News, Virginia.*

Above: One passenger was killed and three others injured early in the morning of October 31, 1948, when the passenger steamer *District of Columbia* was in a collision with the tanker *Georgia* in heavy fog in Hampton Roads, Virginia. The steamer was underway from Old Point Comfort to Norfolk when the collision occurred. Visibility was limited when the tanker was spotted at anchor dead ahead, and the crash occurred. Captain E.H. Eaton said that he had tried to avoid the collision but the strong tide swept the steamer against the tanker. Most of the passengers were at breakfast at the time of the collision and several were thrown to the deck by the crash. **Below:** Ten staterooms on the starboard side of the *District of Columbia* were demolished. *Photos courtesy of the Mariners Museum, Newport News, Virginia.*

Above: The *U.S.S. Missouri*, the Navy's only active battleship at the time, ran aground on Thimble Shoals outside Norfolk, Virginia on January 17, 1950. It was a thoroughly embarrassing situation for the officers and crew of the 57,600 ton ship. The vessel had the nickname "Mighty Mo" and one quick witted news editor coined the phrase: "The Mighty Mo ain't mighty no mo!" **Below:** The Navy decided to dredge a channel behind the battleship to get her back in deep water. The idea did not work. They blasted tunnels under her with high pressure hoses, hired tugs, had several hundred sailors racing from side to side to try to rock her out of the mud. Nothing seemed to free the huge vessel. *Photos courtesy of the National Archives, Washington, D.C.*

CHAPTER EIGHT

One of the more celebrated stories of a vessel aground occurred on January 17, 1950, when the *U.S.S. Missouri*, the Navy's only active battleship at that time, steamed onto Thimble Shoals, just outside Norfolk, Virginia. The famous *BB63* was the flagship of Admiral William F. Halsey during the bombardment of Okinawa on May 28, 1945. The following September she received the Japanese surrender in Tokyo Bay. But the "Mighty Mo" had run aground and was stuck in the Chesapeake Bay mud. The 57,600 ton ship had to be lightened. The operations required extensive dredging and an army of tugboats. Along with the attendant front page publicity, the huge battleship was pulled out of the mud on February 1st and dry-docked to determine any injuries the hull may have suffered while aground. The damage to the ship was light. The greatest injury was done to her officers, by the embarrassment and subsequent courts martial. The salvage was expensive. The cost for dredging, tug boats and beach gear was $130,500. The Navy had to swallow some pride and hire a dredge from the Army to help refloat the *Missouri*. The dry-docking and repairs added another $47,600 to the bill bringing the total cost to $178,100.

On February 18, 1952, two tankers broke in half off Cape Cod Massachusetts in sixty foot seas and a blinding snow storm with winds of near gale force. Coast Guard units converged on the tanker *Fort Mercer* 30 miles off the coast. The tanker *Pendleton* broke up off Provincetown and drifted down the back side of Cape Cod. Early in the evening, a 36-foot motor lifeboat from the Chatham Coast Guard station departed from the fish pier and went out into the storm and rescued 32 of the crewmen from the stern of the wrecked tanker. One man was lost in the rescue effort when he missed the lifeboat, after jumping from a jacob's ladder. The boat returned to Chatham with the survivors and her crew to a hero's welcome. The four men who made the daring rescue: Boatswains mate Bernard C. Webber, Engineer Andrew Fitzgerald, and seamen Richard P. Livesey and Irving Maske, were decorated with the gold lifesaving medal, this nation's highest award for rescue at sea.

The winter of 1951-52 in the North Atlantic seemed to be one continuous storm after another. The ocean was a confusion of weather with gale winds and heavy seas. The storms rose up and as was written in the description of the Leviathan in the Book of Job: "He maketh the deep to boil like a pot; the sea he churns like perfume in a kettle." Ships were disabled all along the coastline. The liners *Queen Mary, America* and the *Ile de France* reported the roughest weather they had ever encountered in the North Atlantic. Dozens of ships reported being in trouble and in need of assistance or delays in arrival. Salvage tugs and Coast Guard Cutters were busy throughout the winter months.

One man fought the sea but he did not win. Captain Hendrik Kurt Carlsen aboard the *Flying Enterprise* on the other side of the Atlantic. When her cargo shifted in the heavy seas the ship developed a heavy port list. The Captain ordered his crew and passengers to abandon ship. They went aboard several other vessels standing nearby to offer aid. The vessel, then listing 60 degrees remained afloat with a crew of one, her master. The tug *Turmoil* standing by, took the *Flying Enterprise* in tow but the Atlantic won the battle. The towline broke fifty miles south of the British Islands and the ship sank. Captain Carlsen was rescued and decorated for upholding the traditions of the sea.

The *U.S.S. Missouri* was refloated during a high spring tide on February 2nd with the use of several tugs hauling with several more alongside, after all of her fuel and ammunition had been off-loaded. *Photo courtesy of the National Archives, Washington, D.C.*

Gale force winds drove the Greek freighter *SS Theafano Livanos* high up on the beach at Cape Henry, Virginia on October 18, 1951. The 4,800 ton vessel lay on the beach for two days. Later, tugs pulled her off and towed her to the shipyard at Newport News for repairs. The hull was damaged extensively. Seventy-six bottom plates were repaired in the shipyard and a new rudder was installed as well as numerous other repairs. *Photo courtesy of the U.S. Coast Guard, Washington, D.C.*

A tragic collision occurred on April 27, 1952, in mid-Atlantic during night maneuvers when the U.S. Naval destroyer-minesweeper *Hobson* was cut in half by the aircraft carrier *Wasp* about 750 miles southeast of Newfoundland. The *Wasp* was conducting flight operations and at about 10 p.m., turned into the wind to recover her aircraft when the accident happened. The destroyer-minesweepers *Hobson* and *Rodman* were at plane guard stations near the carrier. The stations are normally one-half to one mile away from the *Wasp*. The *Hobson* was cut in half as she steamed in front of the aircraft carrier and 176 men went down with their ship. There were only 61 survivors as the *Hobson* sank in only four minutes. On May 26, 1954, an explosion and fire aboard the aircraft carrier *Bennington* killed 103 men and injured 200 more in the Atlantic, 75 miles south of Newport, Rhode Island. The blast was blamed on a faulty catapult mechanism on the deck below the hangar deck. The hangar deck is just below the flight deck. The carrier was steaming north towards Quanset Point Naval Air Station when the explosion occurred. The fire burned for about four hours before being brought under control by the crew. Most of the injured men were brought to hospitals by Navy and Coast Guard helicopters.

Above: The Coast Guard Cutter *Eastwind* alongside the broken stern section of the tanker *SS Fort Mercer*, 30 miles east of Chatham, Cape Cod, Massachusetts on February 18, 1952. A northeast storm with gale winds and sixty foot seas had broken the vessel in half. The Coast Guard cutter took the hulk in tow. **Below:** Coast Guard personnel aboard the cutter *Yakutat* working the rescue of a man on board the forward section of the broken tanker *Fort Mercer*. This wreckage was later sunk with depth charges by the cutter *Unimak*. Photos courtesy of the U.S. Coast Guard, Boston, Massachusetts.

146

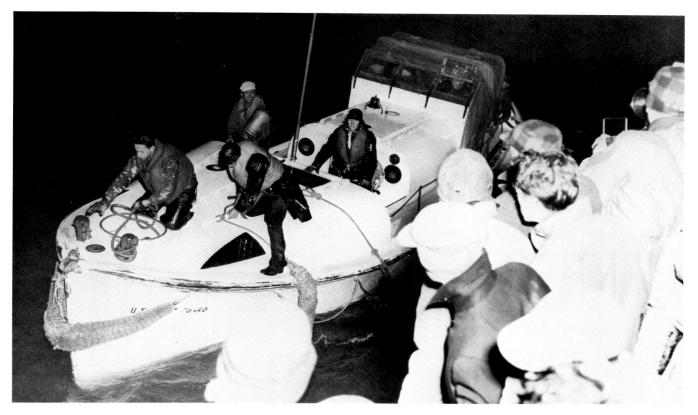

Above: The rescue boat CG 36500 returning to Chatham Fish Pier with her crew of four and thirty-two survivors of the broken tanker *Pendleton* after their incredible rescue at sea, six miles off the coast of Cape Cod. Given the weather conditions at the time, it was considered a miracle that so many were saved. The crew of the lifeboat were awarded the gold lifesaving medal for saving the lives of the imperiled crew of the tanker. **Below:** The stern section of the broken tanker *Pendleton* aground about a mile east of Monomoy Island, south of Cape Cod. This photograph was taken the morning after the rescue of 32 crewmen, who made their way down the Jacob's ladder, shown in the picture, hanging off the stern of the vessel. The men went down the ladder and jumped into the lifeboat during the storm. *Photos by Richard C. Kelsey, Chatham, Massachusetts.*

Above: The freighter *Miget* ran aground off Portsmouth Island during a northeast storm that lashed the coastline on February 3, 1952. The 2,600 ton steamer was driven aground off North Carolina's outer banks. Twenty-six crewmen abandoned the freighter in the ship's lifeboat and while rowing ashore were tipped into the water fifty yards from the beach by the heavy surf. The boat later washed ashore and can be seen on the beach in the background. **Below:** The freighter was pounded to pieces by the surf off shore from Hatteras. It split in two just forward of the stack and was a total loss. *Photos courtesy of the U.S. Coast Guard, Washington, D.C.*

Above: Smoke and flames rose from the blistered hulk of the Norwegian freighter *Black Gull* as it burned sixty miles off Montauk, Long Island, New York on July 19, 1952. The vessel, inbound from Bremen, carried a highly volatile cargo of napthalene and castor oil along with zinc and tin. Three persons burned to death in the fire. Forty-five survivors were picked up by the Swedish-American liner *Gripsholm*. The fire subsided somewhat and the hulk, still smoldering, was towed to New York. She was eventually cut up for scrap. **Below:** The Costa Rican freighter *SS Endeavour* ran aground on a shoal off Cape Henry, Virginia on June 21, 1953 and lay there overnight until the arrival of tugs the next morning. The tugboat *Peerless* tied on to the stern of the grounded freighter and another tug, the *Brant* (not seen in the photo) hauled the *Endeavour* off the shoal as another tug, the *Cherokee* arrived to assist. The coal laden freighter which was bound for Germany, continued on her voyage. *Photos courtesy of the U.S. Coast Guard, Washington, D.C.*

Above: The *Omar Babun*, a 194 foot Honduran freighter came ashore near Rodanthe Beach north of Cape Hatteras, North Carolina on May 14, 1954. Her captain, Jose Villa Diaz, had deliberately run his vessel aground when her cargo shifted and threatened to sink her in the storm. The *Omar Babun* was one day out of Philadelphia bound for Havana with a load of heavy steel machinery when she ran into the violent weather off Hatteras. Some of the heavy steel can be seen on the after part of the ship in the aerial photograph. **Below:** Chief Boatswains Mate Glynn waded into the surf to help one of the crewmen from the grounded freighter as he was hauled ashore by the breeches buoy. The entire crew of fourteen men was rescued in this manner. Coast Guard crews from the Chicamacomico, Oregon Inlet and Cape Hatteras lifeboat stations participated in the rescue of the crewmen from the *Omar Babun*. The wooden vessel was later unloaded and hauled off the beach by salvagers. *Photos courtesy of the U.S. Coast Guard, Washington, D.C.*

150

Above: Three persons were lost when the fishing vessel *Nora V.* out of Wilmington, Delaware capsized on a fishing trip off the coast on July 16, 1954. Ships and planes of the U.S.Coast Guard all joined in a search for survivors. The *CGC Gentian* located the hull of the illfated vessel and the crew rigged lines to haul the boat back to port for salvage. **Below:** The *Student Prince*, a Newfoundland fishing vessel, was disabled in a storm in the Atlantic about 200 miles northeast of Bermuda on January 6, 1955. Her lifeboat had been smashed in an attempt to abandon ship and the vessel was sinking. Her SOS brought the nearest ship, the *SS Queen of Bermuda*, off course. Her skipper spread oil on the rough seas and launched a boat to remove the crew of ten from the *Student Prince.* The *Queen of Bermuda* fell 24 hours behind schedule in making the rescue but was lauded for her efforts. The survivors were landed in Bermuda when the ship docked the next day. *Photos courtesy of the U. S. Coast Guard, Washington, D.C.*

A collision between a ship and a bridge is not an uncommon occurrence but to photograph the event as it happens is unique. On October 5, 1955, the tanker *Fort Fetterman* was bound upstream in the Ashley River near Charleston, South Carolina. It was a nice day and news photographer Richard Burbage was out that morning in a small boat to take routine photographs of river traffic. The sequence of photographs tells the graphic story of the tanker demolishing the west bascule of the open drawbridge. Mr. Burbage had some once-in-a-lifetime photographs which were featured in the Charleston Evening Post. *Photos courtesy of the Charleston Evening Post, Charleston South Carolina.*

Above: The excursion vessel *Pilgrim Belle* which ran between Boston and Provincetown, Massachusetts ran aground in the fog on Spectacle Island in Boston harbor on June 22, 1955. The 272 passengers were taken off by small craft in the harbor and the vessel was eventually refloated, She finished out her summer season in Massachusetts Bay. *Photo courtesy of the Mariners Museum, Newport News, Virginia.* **Below:** The fishing vessel *Shannon* caught fire on December 15, 1955, 35 miles off the New Jersey coast near Cape May. The five crew members were rescued by the trawler *South Seas.* The *CGC Gentian* arrived on scene to try and put out the flames. Foam spray was used to control the blaze but the fire was too far out of control and the vessel burned to her waterline and sank. *Photo courtesy of the U.S. Coast Guard, Washington, D.C.*

Above: On the night of March 15, 1956, off the New England coastline a storm grew to gale force with snow and heavy seas. Soon, conditions deteriorated to blizzard conditions and the 441 foot, 7,000 ton Italian freighter *Etrusco* came ashore at Cedar Point in Scituate, Massachusetts. It was early in the morning on the 16th when the Coast Guard was alerted to the freighter's plight. Rescue conditions were among the worst on record. Heavy seas were breaking over the ship and the wind was gusting to 83 miles per hour. The crew elected to stay on board in the comparative safety of the ship rather than risk transfer. **Below:** At dawn the Coast Guard fired a shot line to the vessel and rigged the breeches buoy. They brought the crew of 30 ashore safely. *Photos courtesy of the U.S. Coast Guard.*

In the early morning hours of March 17, 1956, the Swedish freighter *Nyland* hit the Liberty ship *E. Kirby Smith* as she lie at anchor in Hampton Roads, Virginia. There were no injuries on either vessel. The *Smith* was one of the inactive fleet being used as a grain storage vessel. *Official U.S. Coast Guard Photograph.*

THE ANDREA DORIA/STOCKHOLM COLLISION

Late in the evening of July 25, 1956, the queen of the Italian line, the *Andrea Doria* was steaming towards New York City, fifty miles south of Nantucket Island. The crew and passengers were making plans for the following morning when they would arrive in the city. The Swedish motor vessel *Stockholm* had left New York that day and was sailing east. There were fog banks on the ocean that night. Ships sailed in and out of the fog, making the use of radar a prime necessity.

The reason for the collision has never been positively established and the reading of the radar screen has been questioned on both vessels but the *Stockholm*, with an extra strong bow for plowing through ice-filled northern European waters, sliced into the starboard side of the *Andrea Doria* just below the bridge. The bow of the *Stockholm* penetrated a third of the way through the forward section of the *Doria* and unfortunately, hit the empty fuel tanks in the lower decks filling them with sea water and causing the liner to take an immediate starboard list.

It was 11:09 p.m. and by midnight, radios were broadcasting the messages throughout the New England area. Every ship within 100 miles of the accident raced to the scene. With the mild conditions, it was one of the better rescue operations at sea as other ships took on most of the 1,709 passengers and crew from the stricken liner. But, fiftytwo died, either on board the crippled ship at the time of the collision or in the fog shrouded waters. For eleven hours, the Italian liner stayed afloat. At 10:09 a.m. on the following day, the *Andrea Doria* turned over and sank in 225 feet of water where she rests today.   It is ironic, however, that this should ever have happened. And, but for international laws governing the sea, the *Andrea Doria* might have been saved. When the Coast Guard cutter *Hornbeam* arrived on scene, early in the morning, she wanted to take the ship in tow to shallow waters so that if she sank, she would rest on the bottom with most of the hull above water. Salvage in that position would have been relatively easy and only a matter of days or weeks. There was a shoal nearby where the water was only 70 feet deep. Without a release for the responsibility of the ship (she was foreign registry) the *Hornbeam* could not put a line aboard the stricken vessel. About 9:30 a.m., the word came through granting permission for the tow but by then it was too late. The main deck was under water and it was the beginning of the end of the ocean liner. The Captain and the last remaining crewmen came aboard the *Hornbeam* and were brought ashore, sad, but alive.

ABOVE: Late at night on July 25, 1956, about fifty miles south of Nantucket Island, the Swedish motor vessel *Stockholm* collided with the Italian liner *Andrea Doria* in dense fog. This photograph was made about nine a.m. the next morning. BELOW: The *Stockholm* hit the *Andrea Doria* on just under the bridge and the *Doria* took a starboard list which deteriorated until she sank about eleven on the morning of the 26th. The heavy list made it impossible to launch lifeboats on the port side. *Photos courtesy of the U.S. Coast Guard.*

Above: The Coast Guard Cutter *Hornbeam* was on scene the next morning. The crew of the *Andrea Doria* went aboard the cutter. Fiftytwo persons died in the collision but sixteen hundred and sixty-two people were rescued by Naval, Coast Guard, and Merchant vessels. **Below:** The bow of the Swedish liner *Stockholm* suffered heavy damage. Military helicopters carried injured passengers to shoreside hospitals for treatment. *Photos courtesy of the U.S. Coast Guard.*

Above: The 29-million dollar Italian liner *Andrea Doria* turned on her beam ends just prior to sinking, 45 miles south of Nantucket Island. An empty lifeboat drifted nearby. **Below:** The ship begins her final plunge to the bottom. The unused port lifeboats floated away, upside down. *Photos courtesy of the U.S. Coast Guard.*

The *Andrea Doria* turned over and took her final plunge to the bottom of the ocean at about 11 a.m. on July 26, 1956. She lies in 225 feet of water. This was a Pulitzer Prize winning photograph, taken by Harry Trask, copyright to the Boston Herald Traveler. *Photo courtesy of Harry Trask.*

Above: The crew of the *Helga Bolten* stand at the ship's stern rail waiting for life rafts sent over by the Coast Guard Cutter *Chincoteague.* The 10,600 ton vessel was hit by a storm on October 29, 1956, while carrying a cargo of coal to Bergen, Norway. High winds and heavy seas smashed her two forward holds and she called for help as her pumps could not handle the flooding in the holds. The vessel lay 400 miles southeast of Cape Race, Newfoundland and was in danger of sinking. **Below:** The crew of the *Helga Bolten* in two life rafts were picked up by the Coast Guard Cutter and returned to Norfolk, Virginia. The stricken vessel did not sink. The ship was towed to the Azores by two salvage tugs. She was repaired and later returned to sea. *Photos courtesy of the U.S. Coast Guard, Washington, D.C.*

In the early years of development, aviation became an important arm of the Coast Guard. Surfmen from the Kill Devil Hills Lifeboat Station at Cape Hatteras, North Carolina served as an amateur ground crew for the Wright Brothers when they made their famous flight in December, 1903. In the annual report of the Coast Guard for the fiscal year ending June 30, 1920, a reference to aviation appears:

"The application of aviation to the uses of the Coast Guard in the saving of life and property from the perils of the sea, in the locating of floating derelicts along our coasts, and in the rendering of other kindred service can now be regarded as an assured proposition. A Coast Guard aviation station has been established at Morehead City, N.C., at practically no expense to the service. The buildings and equipment were acquired from the Navy Department. The aircraft in use are the Navy H-S flying boats. The station is conducting experiments with the view of furthering the effectiveness of aircraft to life and property saving purposes. As funds become available it is proposed to establish similar stations elsewhere. It is earnestly recommended that Congress give its support to the development of this activity of the Coast Guard. A number of officers of the Coast Guard are already qualified pilots of aircraft. During the World War, officers of the Coast Guard on aviation duty were assigned to command naval air stations, as test pilots, as inspectors of aeronautic engineering material, and as patrol and instructing pilots and technical specialists.

"It is of interest to note that Lieut. Commander Elmer F. Stone, United States Coast Guard, was first pilot on the trans-Atlantic seaplane NC-4."

In the ensuing years, the pilots of the Coast Guard shared the designs and developments of Navy amphibious aircraft. This worked to advantage and in July 1949, the Grumman Aircraft Company began to produce a twin engine amphibious aircraft for the Navy and Air Force that would ultimately become the primary search and rescue aircraft for the U.S. Coast Guard. The capabilities of the Albatross were quickly recognized by the Coast Guard and on May 7, 1951, the first plane was delivered to the Air Station at Brooklyn, New York. The plane was officially designated as the HU-16E. A total of 88 aircraft saw service in the Coast Guard over a period of thirty-three years. The plane participated in a multitude of missions. The reliability of the aircraft was outstanding in search and rescue, and law enforcement missions.

Progress, however, does not stand still. In 1972, new modern helicopters with space age technology took over the rescue operations at sea and the Albatross was assigned to long range patrols along the east coast surveying the foreign fishing fleets from the Grand Banks to the Caribbean. The plane also maintained a watch over the off-shore waters for drug smugglers. The long outstanding record of the aircraft came to an end on March 10, 1983, when the last amphibian plane in Government service was retired with appropriate honors at the Coast Guard Air Station on Cape Cod, Massachusetts. The last plane, number 7250, now rests with distinction at the entrance to the Cape Cod Air Station on permanent display.

The HU-16E Albatros flying boat.

Above: Ten men were lost in the collision between the 4,500 ton Liberian freighter *Elna II* and the 16,350 ton American tanker *Mission San Francisco*. The accident occurred on March 7 1957 at 12:30 a.m. in pea soup fog on the Delaware River below Wilmington. An explosion following the crash shattered the tanker and sank her. In the photograph the freighter is shown with a smashed bow and in the background the tanker lies still smoldering. The freighter was moving south with a crew of 22 and a pilot. The tanker was proceeding northward enroute to Philadelphia. *Photo courtesy of the Mariners Museum, Newport News, Virginia.* **Below:** The New York sight-seeing boat *City of Keansburg* ran aground while approaching the dock at the Statue of Liberty in New York Harbor on May 24, 1957. Two Coast Guard cutters and other craft went to her aid. There were 150 passengers on board. With a rising tide, she was freed after a short time and tied up at the docks. There were no damages or injuries and the extra excitement was probably amusing to those on board. *Photo courtesy of the U.S. Coast Guard, New York, N.Y.*

Above: A collision in the early morning fog just outside Newport, Rhode Island harbor took seventeen lives and injured thirty-six. On the morning of August 7, 1958, the *SS Gulfoil*, was sailing in ballast from Providence, R.I. to Port Arthur, Texas. The *SS Graham* was headed into Newport harbor with a million gallons of gasoline aboard when the *Gulfoil* loomed out of the fog and struck the *Graham* on the port bow just aft of the forecastle. A huge fire erupted immediately and engulfed both vessels. **Below:** Navy and Coast Guard vessels rushed to the scene and began to fight the fires aboard the *Graham*. *Photos courtesy of the U.S. Coast Guard, Washington, D.C.*

Above: The crew of the *Graham* abandoned ship. Navy and Coast Guard cutters from nearby bases rushed to the scene to fight the flames which at times, towered high into the air. **Below:** Navy firemen wearing asbestos suits boarded the *SS Graham* and fought the flames close up with foam. The fire burned for five hours before it was brought under control. *Photos courtesy of the U.S. Coast Guard, Washington, D.C.*

Above: The Norwegian freighter *Belleville* went on the rocks off Brenton Point, Rhode Island on September 24, 1957. The vessel was bound from Boston with a cargo of tin, rubber and tapioca, for Philadelphia. The mistake in navigation occurred in clear weather and when the tide dropped, the vessel fractured. **Below:** The center portion of the ship was hard on the rocks but her bow section was afloat. Later, rough weather split the hull into two pieces. Most of her cargo was recovered but the ship was a total loss. *Photos by John T. Hopf, Newport, Rhode Island.*

Above: It is an old Portuguese custom. When their ships are beyond salvage, they set them afire. Such was the case on September 7, 1958, when the fishing vessel *Ana Maria* was set on fire, 160 miles south of Cape Race, Newfoundland. Her crew had been removed by another fishing vessel nearby. When the Coast Guard cutter *Spencer* answering an SOS call, arrived on scene, the old schooner was in flames from stem to stern. The hulk of the vessel was sunk by the *Spencer* with gunfire as she was a menace to navigation. **Below:** The 22,340 ton Liberian tanker *African Queen* struck a shoal off Ocean City, Maryland and broke in half on December 30, 1958 during a storm. The crew of 47 were all rescued by nine helicopters from the Navy, Coast Guard and Marine Corps. The rescue was made by air because the sea conditions at the time were too rough for surface craft. The tanker was bound from Columbia, South America, with crude oil, for Paulsboro, New Jersey. The photograph was taken on December 31st. The broken sections of the vessel lay on a sand bar eleven miles east of Ocean City, Maryland. *Photos courtesy of the U.S. Coast Guard, Washington, D.C.*

Above: Ship collisions sometimes create remarkable situations for news photographs. Two American vessels were in collision 22 miles east of Atlantic City, New Jersey at 3 a.m. on March 26, 1959. The passenger ship *Santa Rosa* ran into the stern of the tanker *Valchem* carrying away her stack and ventilators on the bow of the liner. A Coast Guard helicopter hovered over the *Santa Rosa* to hoist a critically injured seaman for removal to an Atlantic City hospital. The liner carried 247 passengers and a crew of 265. **Below:** The tanker *Valchem* with a deep hole in her stern. The collision caused flooding of the lower engine room and resultant loss of power. One crewman from the tanker was killed. Three others were missing and presumed lost, and sixteen were injured. Commercial tugs towed the tanker to port. *Photos courtesy of the U.S. Coast Guard, Washington, D.C.*

Above: In the East River, New York City, the tanker *Empress Bay* sank under the Manhattan bridge on June 25, 1958, after she collided with the Swedish freighter *Nebraska* in the early morning hours. Two tanker crewmen were lost but 49 people were saved. There was 280,000 gallons of gasoline aboard the tanker, which ignited on impact. This spread a blanket of fire on the water that engulfed both vessels and endangering waterfront areas on the Manhattan and Brooklyn sides of the river as well as the bridge. The tanker was later raised by commercial salvage operations on September 9, 1958. **Below:** The World War II Liberty ship *Antonin Dvorak* was being towed as a dead ship to Baltimore, Maryland, when she broke loose in a storm and grounded at Avon, North Carolina on the outer banks. The vessel came ashore on March 28, 1959. She was refloated on April 22nd and resumed the tow to Baltimore. *Photos courtesy of the U.S. Coast Guard, Washington, D.C.*

A disaster occurred on December 21, 1960, 125 miles east of Cape Hatteras, North Carolina. Gale winds and high seas broke the T-2 tanker *Pine Ridge* into two pieces shortly before noon and seven men were lost in the accident. The stern section of the tanker wallowed in heavy seas 125 miles east of Cape Hatteras with the 29 surviving crew members. Twenty-eight of these men were taken off the stern by helicopters from the Navy aircraft carrier *Valley Forge*. The Chief engineer, John Richart, 36, of Wilmington, Delaware remained on board the stern for the long tow to Newport News by commercial tugs. The *Pine Ridge* was the eleventh T-2 tanker to break in half. Forty-one lives had been lost in previous accidents of these type ships. On December 23rd, the surviving crew members reached shore thankful to be alive and critical of the seaworthiness of their ship. One crewman, Robert Gill of Monterey, Mexico told of the shock to the crew when the ship broke up in seas that would normally be of no threat to a vessel of that size. *Photo courtesy of the U.S. Coast Guard.*

170

CHAPTER NINE

As the twentieth century moved ahead, the shipwrecks continued. No man is perfect, and ships are built and sailed by men. In modern technology, the extent of progress realized is usually measured by the degree of success achieved. New procedures in sea rescue were put forth in the 1960s with space age electronics using computers. At first the operations were limited to the north Atlantic but the success in the program caused it to be instituted world wide. The system was dubbed AMVER. The acronym is a term for Automated Mutual-assistance VEssel Rescue. It is a computer, able to calculate the locations of merchant vessels on the ocean where ever they might be needed in an emergency. The computer is advised of the nature and location where help is needed and it quickly identifies the names and locations of nearby ships.

It is an ages old tradition of the sea to aid fellow mariners. Often a ship in an emergency situation is all alone at sea when help might be just over the horizon. The new computer brings help where none was thought to exist. The system can also aid overseas aircraft when the need arises. If an airliner is crippled and has to ditch in the ocean, the computer can advise the pilot the location of the nearest ships where the rescue of passengers can be expedited after ditching.

The AMVER center is in New York City. The computer is advised daily of ship locations which are flashed in by radio communications. There are more than 70 cooperating radio stations around the world. Varying information is available: eastbound or westbound ships, those carrying doctors, locations of derelicts and their drift, locations of icebergs in the north Atlantic and weather information which enables ships at sea to change course to avoid severe storms. The program plots the locations of all ships participating to aid in search and rescue operations. The program is free of cost to all ships and their companies.

The jet age brought some unique problems to ships in New York harbor. Vessels passing through Riker's Island channel were in danger of collisions with air liners landing at LaGuardia airport. Cargo ships at that time had masts and booms that towered over 100 feet in the air and low flying aircraft, on approach to land at LaGuardia were in danger of colliding with the ships passing in the channel. A quick solution was devised when the operators of the Port of New York agreed to telephone the control tower at LaGuardia prior to passage of vessels through the channel to avoid any accidents. The situation has almost been eliminated today as most merchant ships carry their cargo in containers and tall masts are no longer needed on board ships.

A fire charred the nation's largest aircraft carrier on December 19, 1960. The *U.S.S. Constellation*, still under construction, burned for twelve hours before being brought under control. At mid-morning, a lift truck on the hangar deck ruptured a plug on a full 500 gallon fuel tank. The liquid gushed out and ran down an elevator shaft as a welder was working. The blaze ran quickly to other decks engulfing wooden scaffolding and other equipment. Fifty workmen died in the ten alarm fire and over 100 were injured. The damage to the ship, which was nearing completion, was about 75 million dollars.

The worst submarine disaster in U.S. Naval history occurred on April 10, 1963 when the atomic submarine *Thresher* was lost during deep diving tests in the Atlantic, 220 miles east of Cape Cod. The sub made her last dive at 9 o'clock in water 8,400 feet deep. There were 129 men aboard the vessel. There were 96 enlisted men, 16 Naval officers and 17 civilians technicians from Portsmouth, N.H. Navy Yard. Recently overhauled at Portsmouth, the *Thresher* was accompanied by the submarine rescue ship *Skylark* which lost contact with the submarine after the dive. Any hope of rescue was abandoned as the depth at which the *Thresher* lay would crush the hull. The *Thresher* was a nuclear attack submarine launched in 1960 and was 278 feet long and cost 45 million dollars.

Above: The overturned bow of the tanker *Pine Ridge*. This part of the tanker contains more than two thirds of the vessel's 523-foot length with over 300-feet hidden underwater. This section sank on the night of the 22nd. **Below:** The 441-foot freighter *Marine Merchant* broke in half just forward of the bridge while battling heavy seas in the Gulf of Maine on April 14, 1961. The crew abandoned the vessel early in the morning and they were picked up by other merchant ships answering the SOS. The freighter sank about 10 a.m. The cause of the accident was attributed to improper loading of a bulk sulphur cargo. *Photos courtesy of the U.S. Coast Guard, Washington, D.C.*

Above: A huge Atlantic storm disabled several ships at sea and broke the tanker *Gem* in half on March 8, 1962. When the tanker broke, there were eight men on the forward section and one of these was killed trying to launch a lifeboat. In the photograph, the stern section of the vessel has her name painted on deck with the words "27 MEN" to denote to rescue aircraft their plight. The 34 men were rescued off both sections of the ship and brought safely ashore. The two sections of the tanker were towed to Jacksonville, Florida, by salvage vessels. **Below:** Winter on the North Atlantic bodes ill for the poor fishermen. Sheathed in ice, the dragger *Katie D.* lays grounded on Rocky Neck off Gloucester, Massachusetts on December 31, 1962. The vessel lost power and drifted ashore in a severe winter storm. Eight crewmen were rescued by the Coast Guard. The dragger was a total loss. *Photos courtesy of the U.S. Coast Guard, Washington, D.C.*

Above: In the annals of shipwrecks there are many that are listed as "Went missing". On February 3, 1963, the 523-foot tanker *SS Marine Sulphur Queen* departed Beaumont, Texas with a crew of 39 persons and a cargo of molten sulphur. The vessel was due to arrive at Norfolk, Virginia at noon on February 7th. There were no communications or sightings of the vessel and she disappeared without a trace. Later, evidence of the tragedy was located in waters off the coast of Florida when articles identified with the missing ship were located during an extensive search in February and March. Some of the articles shown in the photograph included an eight-foot piece of the quarterboard, eight life jackets, some torn by sharks, five life rings, one shirt, an oil can, gasoline can, a cone buoy and a fog horn. *Photo courtesy of the U.S. Coast Guard, Washington, D.C.* **Below:** The United States Navy Minesweeper *Grouse* ran aground on Little Salvage Reef, a rocky ledge about two miles off Rockport, Massachusetts, early in the morning of September 21, 1963. Eleven crewmen were rescued by the Coast Guard when heavy seas built up and threatened the vessel. Several refloating efforts were tried but the 136-foot vessel was a total loss and the hull was later stripped and burned. *Photo courtesy of the U.S. Naval Photographic Center, Washington, D.C.*

174

Above: On March 1, 1964, the Liberian tanker *Amphialos* was fighting a fierce storm in the North Atlantic when the vessel broke in half. The bow section sank. The stern half was taken in tow by the salvage tug *Curb* of the Merritt, Chapman and Scott Company of New York. The tow was futile, however, as the ship sank about 250 miles east of Boston, Massachusetts.
Below: The 440-foot bow section of the Norwegian tanker *M.V. Stolt Dagali* was towed by the tug *Cynthia Moran* (not shown), toward New York City, off the northern New Jersey coast on November 27, 1964. The bow section was escorted to New York by the Coast Guard cutter *Cape Strait*. The 582-foot, 12,723 ton tanker was in collision with the Israeli luxury liner *Shalom*, on Thanksgiving day, November 26th, 46 miles southeast of New York. The 140-foot stern section of the tanker sank immediately after the collision. The 23,000 ton *Shalom* received a forty foot long gash on her starboard side as a result of the collision. *Photos courtesy of the U.S. Coast Guard.*

Above: The North Atlantic is cold and cruel. Crewmen from the sinking fishing vessel *Maureen & Michael* were rescued by a rubber life raft in the rough waters east of Newfoundland on February 23, 1967. The fishing vessel had been heavily damaged in the heavy seas and her crew had fought for three days to save her. The Coast Guard cutter *Castle Rock* arrived on scene and removed the eight crewmen just before their vessel went down. **Below:** On April 2, 1967, a Russian crewman was seriously injured aboard the Soviet Factory vessel *Grigory Lysenko*, 70 miles south of Montauk Point, Long Island, New York. The Captain of the large vessel radioed for medical assistance. A United States Coast Guard helicopter was dispatched and landed on the rear deck. The injured seaman was transferred to the Public Health Service Hospital on Staten Island, New York. *Photos courtesy of the U.S. Coast Guard.*

Early on the morning of March 3, 1968 the Liberian oil tanker *Ocean Eagle* ran aground just outside the entrance to the channel into San Juan harbor in Puerto Rico. Heavy seas pushed the tanker against the rocky shoals and she split in half spilling more than two million gallons of crude oil into the harbor fouling beaches and wildlife. Thirty-three Greek crewmen were rescued by tugboats in the area. The U.S. Navy undertook the job of salvage and removal of the wrecked ship and one month later was successful in clearing the entrance to the harbor. *Official Photograph of the U.S. Navy.*

Above: The *District of Columbia*, the last of the old Bay Liners fell victim to a fire on the afternoon of June 4, 1969. The fire, believed to be arson, engulfed the old wooden vessel and at one time it was feared that the old steamer would sink at her berth at Pier 3, Pratt Street in Baltimore, Maryland. The ship had last operated as the *Provincetown* and during her long lay-up at Baltimore, vandals had devastated her interior, smashing mirrors and paneling. Her future was to be as a floating restaurant but the fire damaged her beyond repair. *Photo courtesy of the Mariners Museum, Newport News, Virginia.* **Below:** On the outer banks of North Carolina, the trawler *Oriental* ran aground in a storm and broke up in heavy surf on Oregon Inlet Beach near Nags Head on December 21, 1969. Three men on board the 85-foot fishing vessel were hoisted to safety by an HH-52 amphibious helicopter from the Coast Guard air station at Elizabeth City, North Carolina. *Photo by Aycock Brown of Manteo, N.C. courtesy of the U.S. Coast Guard, Washington, D.C.*

World War II had been over for ten years but its vestiges were still having an effect. A tragic accident occurred on July 23, 1965, off the coast of North Carolina when the Maine fishing vessel *Snoopy* was destroyed by an exploding torpedo. The *Snoopy* was fishing with a group of vessels out of New Bedford, Massachusetts. Captain Edward Doodley of Portland, Maine had spoken by radio with Captain Norman Maillett of the trawler *Prowler* and had told him that he had "something in the bag net" and was checking it. Captain Maillett said he could see a long round object swaying in the net over the midsection of the *Snoopy*. He added "It apparently hit something, there was a big bang followed by smoke, then there wasn't a ship."

Only four men from a crew of twelve survived the blast and were picked up, badly injured, from the water by the surrounding boats. The survivors, all from Maine, were: Peter Leavitt, the mate, Richard Lindahl, a deck hand, Harold Martin the cook and Leland French, also a deck hand. Only one body, that of Captain Doodley was recovered. For two days and nights the Coast Guard units searched the area for survivors but none was found. The fishing ground where the explosion occurred was a graveyard for Allied shipping during World War II and was the area referred to as Torpedo Junction, because of the many ships sunk by German U-boats during the war. Two weeks later a New England trawler pulled up another torpedo in her net fifty miles east of Virginia. This time the fishermen returned the missile to the bottom of the ocean and marked it with a buoy. The Navy sent demolition experts out and they disarmed the torpedo.

The primary function of the early Revenue Cutter Service in 1790 was the prevention of smuggling. When the Cutter Service joined with the Life Saving service and became the Coast Guard they once again had to fight the smuggled goods during the period of prohibition. Today the Coast Guard is fighting a new war on drug smugglers. The pattern is similar to the rum runners but the cargo is worth ten times what whiskey was worth. Millions of dollars and expensive yachts are involved in the illicit trade. The various coves and secluded inlets along the Atlantic Coast provide an easy hiding place for the boats to lie low and escape detection. The Coast Guard continues the battle to suppress the traffic in contraband drugs but as with the liquor war, for every one caught, ten more escape.

On November 12, 1965 the 5,000 ton liner *Yarmouth Castle* cast off her lines from the pier at Miami, Florida and began a cruise to Nassau through the straits of Florida. Aboard were 550 passengers and crewmen. The ship sailed around the Great Bahama bank into the northeast Providence channel. The weather was perfect and the night was bright with the moon casting a reflection in the tropical waters.

Just after midnight, fire erupted on the upper deck forward and burned out of control. The flames spread throughout the ship rapidly as many of the passengers and crewmen abandoned the vessel in lifeboats. Another cruise ship, the *Bahama Star* was nearby and pulled near the burning liner to help those trying to escape the flames. Many passengers were forced to jump from the blazing decks into the ocean in only their nightclothes. The *Bahama Star* launched her lifeboats to pick up the passengers who were in the water swimming away from the fire. Witnesses said that the ship was a mass of flames from bow to stern. Another ship, the *Finnpulp* ran alongside the *Yarmouth Castle* and removed more passengers from the deck. When her paint started to blister and smoke, her Captain pulled away and resumed picking up more people from the water.

The flaming ship rolled over and sank soon after. The two rescue ships saved a total of 462 persons. It was estimated that 88 perished in the fire and some may have been lost in the water. Thirty four persons were transferred to the Princess Margaret hospital at Nassau when the *Bahama Star* docked. One man died at the hospital and 14 persons who were badly burned were airlifted by Coast Guard helicopter to Miami. Claims were filed, following the accident, against the shipping line in excess of fifty million dollars. The Coast Guard investigation placed heavy blame on Captain Voutsinas and the officers of the *Yarmouth Castle*.

The Chesapeake Bay Bridge and Tunnel was closed on January 21, 1970 when a Navy cargo ship broke loose in 50-mile per hour winds. The 14,000 ton *Yancey* swept away five sections of the two-lane roadway and the supporting pilings. The bridge-tunnel complex was closed for two months while repairs were completed at a cost of two and one half million dollars. *Photo by Tamte-Wilson Photography, Norfolk, Virginia.*

CHAPTER TEN

American technology advanced with the opening of the Chesapeake Bay Bridge-Tunnel to traffic on April 15, 1964, following three and a half years of construction. The two hundred million dollar project connected Cape Charles on the southern end of the Delmarva Peninsula, across the entrance to Chesapeake Bay to the city of Norfolk. The 17.6 mile crossing time was reduced from a two hour ferry ride to twentyfive minutes by automobile. The complex boasted of twelve miles of trestles and two mile-long tunnels, two bridges, two miles of causeway and four man-made islands. The advertising invited one to "Go to sea in your car", which in reality was true. It is very pleasant to drive among the ocean-going ships while motoring from north to south along the Atlantic coastline.

In January 1970, the Chesapeake Bay Bridge-Tunnel was closed down for six weeks when a Navy cargo ship dragged her anchors in high winds and smashed into the southern end of the roadway two miles from shore. Five sections of the two lane roadway and pilings were knocked down by the *U.S.S. Yancey* when 50 m.p.h. winds drove her from her anchorage. No one was injured in the accident, either on the ship or the bridge but the closing had a damaging effect on the economy of the peninsula. The tourists, unable to continue their southern route took the long way around through Richmond, Virginia. The bridge-tunnel complex carried over 3,000 vehicles and over 9,000 people each day. The loss of this business was devastating to the economy of the peninsula. Motels, restaurants and other related industries suffered greatly in the closing.

The U. S. Navy, anxious to ease the economic impact, began an emergency ferry service with four landing craft and provided helicopter service across the bay for persons on urgent business. But this did not placate the angry residents or the eastern shore businessmen. The loss of revenue to the Bridge Tunnel complex was estimated to be $600,000. Repairs were completed and the complex was reopened on March 4, 1970. The total cost of repairs was approximately $2,500,000. The U.S. Government paid 90% of the damages. The insurance company for the Chesapeake Bay Bridge-Tunnel complex paid $150,000 and the company had to pay almost $100,000. Following the accident, navigation rules were amended by the Coast Guard in 1974 designed to protect the Chesapeake Bay Bridge-Tunnel against future accidents of this type. The new rules spelled out conditions under which vessels could anchor, pass and navigate the waters surrounding the complex. The new order was dated August 30, 1974 and was signed by Admiral O.W. Siler, Commandant, U.S. Coast Guard.

The responsibility of a ship is with her Captain. But when the ship is wrecked, the owners take the losses. To prevent financial ruin, the owners buy insurance on their ships. This is to prevent being put out of business in case the ship is sunk or wrecked. The name synonymous with marine insurance is Lloyds of London. For over three hundred years, this insurance exchange has covered the risks and been the principal anchor in maritime underwriting. It all began in a 17th century London Coffeehouse on Tower Street near the Thames River. The English have a penchant for tradition and many practices begun at Lloyds in the early days are carried on today. Assistants working on the underwriting floor are still referred to as "Waiters" after their predecessors in the coffeehouse.

Lloyds is an association of underwriters. The term "underwriter" comes from the early "risk takers" writing their names one under the other on the insurance policy. The underwriters today insure ships, airplanes, space satellites, professional athletes and movie stars. Lloyds is now on Lime Street in London's financial district. Clerks continue to use quills to enter ships casualties in the ledgers. The Lloyd's Register of Shipping is a list of ships the world over. It is an independent classification society, not directly connected with the insurance firm however a close liaison is maintained with them by joint memberships in both societies.

The tug *Maryland* sank in high winds and heavy seas on December 18, 1971 in North Carolina's Albemarle Sound. Six men were lost in the accident and only one man was saved. John Williams, 61, of Norfolk, Virginia was rescued by the yacht *Georgetta* and then taken by Coast Guard helicopter to Albemarle Hospital in Elizabeth City. Williams told investigators that the barge ran the tug down during a stop to lengthen the towing line because of the weather conditions. *Photo Courtesy of the U.S. Coast Guard.*

Above: The Norwegian cargo ship *Thordis Presthus* was torn by explosions and fires on January 18, 1970 while underway, about 85 miles off Wilmington, North Carolina. Two crewmen were killed and eight were injured fighting the fires. The communications equipment was disabled completely. A passing tugboat spotted the glow in the sky and radioed the Coast Guard. They brought the fire under control. The survivors were taken off and landed at Morehead City, North Carolina. For a week the fire continued to reflash and was extinguished each time. The freighter was finally brought into Norfolk, Virginia with a heavy port list. The damage to the vessel and loss of cargo was more than two million dollars. The ship was towed to Germany and cut up for scrap. **Below:** The Atlantic Ocean has an approximate area of 33,420,000 square miles, which would seem to be ample for the ships that sail on it. But on September 14, 1972, the 14,458 ton American containership *Transhawaii* ran into the portside of the 12,000 ton Columbian freighter *Republica de Columbia*, twelve miles east of Cape Hatteras, North Carolina near the Diamond Shoals Light Station. Four men were injured in the crash and one man was killed. The Captain of the *Republica de Columbia* said that his rudder stuck on the port side causing his ship to veer in front of the container vessel. An estimated 24,000 gallons of diesel oil spilled from the Columbian freighter but was dissipated in the ocean. *Photos courtesy of the U.S. Coast Guard, Washington, D.C.*

Above: Following a collision, New York City fire department boats, together with Coast Guard units worked in the early morning hours of June 2, 1973, to extinguish the blaze which left the *C.V. Sea Witch*, a smoldering hulk. **Below:** The *Sea Witch* was outbound from New York when it rammed the tanker *Esso Brussels* while she lay at anchor with a full load of crude oil aboard. The fire that followed cost 16 lives and turned the two vessels into piles of blackened steel. *Photos courtesy of the U.S. Coast Guard.*

Above: The Greek oil tanker *Elias* exploded and split in half alongside the pier at Philadelphia on April 9, 1974 while her cargo of 216,000 barrels of heavy asphalt oil was being unloaded. The explosion killed ten men and the tanker sank in the Delaware River beside the pier. There were other ships close by, but they were towed away and thus avoided damage in the huge fire. Thirteen crewmen aboard the *Elias* were injured and were taken to area hospitals. *Photo courtesy of the U.S. Coast Guard, Washington, D.C.* **Below:** The Soviet research vessel *Belogorsk* ran up on a stone jetty in Woods Hole, Massachusetts on September 3, 1974. The ship was in port to take part in a cooperative fisheries program with United States scientists. She was assisted off the rocks without damage by the Coast Guard tug *Towline* and tied up at a nearby pier. *Photo by the Author.*

Above: Fire broke out in the engine room of the British cruise ship *Cunard Ambassador* 40 miles off Key West, Florida early on the morning of September 12, 1974. The vessel was en-route from Port Everglades, Florida to New Orleans Louisiana to pick up passengers for a Caribbean cruise. None of the 290 crew members was injured. **Below:** Coast Guard cutters from Key West went to the aid of the stricken liner and fought the fire for three days before bringing it under control. *Photos courtesy of the U.S. Coast Guard, Washington, D.C.*

Above: The Liberian tanker *Spartan Lady* broke up in heavy seas 150 miles south of Martha's Vineyard Island on April 4, 1975. The crew gathered on the after part of the stern. Coast Guard helicopters arrived to rescue them as the rough seas tossed their half ship around. **Below:** The bow section floated away from the stern and had to be sunk by gunfire as it was a menace to navigation. The cargo of 500,000 gallons of oil was lost at sea. *Photos courtesy of the U.S. Coast Guard.*

Above: The Japanese freighter *Musashino Maru* went aground in a heavy rain squall at Searsport, Maine early in the morning of February 2, 1976. Her bottom was holed by the rocks on the shore and the vessel was high and dry at low tide. She was ashore for twelve days and was finally pulled off and towed to a shipyard for repairs. *Photo by Bob Beattie, Belfast, Maine.*
Below: On April 1, 1976, the 83 foot fishing trawler *Lady Barbara* grounded in Great Machipango Inlet on the Atlantic Ocean side of the Eastern Shore of Virginia. A helicopter from Elizabeth City was dispatched with pumps but before it arrived, the fishing vessel sank. Seven crewmen on board had been taken off by another fishing boat. *Photo courtesy of the U.S. Coast Guard, Washington, D.C.*

The New Bedford fishing vessel *Sylvester F. Whalen* came ashore on Cisco Beach on Nantucket Island, Massachusetts, on November 4, 1976. The 91-foot vessel was returning from Georges Bank offshore and had developed a bad leak. Electrical power was lost and when pumps could not keep her afloat, the Captain decided to beach his vessel. The Coast Guard removed the crew of six by helicopter and the boat was a total loss. *Photo by Jeff Barnard, Nantucket, Mass.*

The concerns by environmentalists about oil spills by ocean going tankers were intensified in 1967 when the supertanker *Torrey Canyon* grounded and broke in two off Lands End, the southwestern point of the British Islands. Millions of gallons of crude oil washed up on the beaches of Cornwall. The ecological damage was in the millions of dollars and headlines all over the world publicized the event. The accident was a harbinger of many more to come. In 1968, two gasoline barges collided off Staten Island in New York and burned. In 1969, an offshore oil well blow-out at Santa Barbara in California coated beaches with crude oil. In December, the tanker *Keo* broke in half in the stormy north Atlantic and the ship went down with all hands. In February 1970, the tanker *Arrow* grounded in Chedabucto Bay in Nova Scotia and broke in half fouling the entire bay with oil.

In January 1971, the tanker *Esso Gettysburg* grounded near New Haven and spilled 385,000 gallons of fuel oil in Long Island sound. The accidents continued year after year. Explosions on empty tankers were another danger for mariners. In January 1975, a collision at Marcus Hook, Pennsylvania resulted in a huge fire on board the tanker *Corinthos*. In 1976, the United States celebrated its bicentennial year and in December, the tanker *Sansenina* exploded at an oil terminal at San Pedro, California and eight persons were killed. At the same time on the Atlantic Coast the Liberian tanker *Argo Merchant* ran up on the Nantucket Shoals 29 miles southeast of the island and six days later broke in two spilling seven and a half million gallons of bunker oil into the Atlantic ocean. Ten days later the Liberian tanker *Olympic Games* grounded off New Jersey spilling more oil on the beaches. A few days later the Panamanian tanker *Grand Zenith* with a 38 man crew and eight million gallons of oil disappeared in the north Atlantic. The accidents have abated somewhat but it was the worst ten year period for oil spills in history except for World War II off Cape Hatteras, North Carolina.

Among the United States exports to foreign countries are pesticides. This business is closely regulated by numerous government agencies because the toxic properties of the ingredients pose a health hazard to human beings. Extreme care must be exercised in the handling of these chemicals. In February 1979, an emergency arose when the container ship *Maria Costa* sustained underwater hull damage in heavy seas while passing the Azores. The punctured hull resulted in flooding in a hold containing sixty-five tons of Mocap 10G, stowed on pallets. The active chemical in the pesticide was poison and hazardous to humans through inhalation, ingestion or absorption through the skin. In addition the chemicals were toxic to marine life. The hold was flooded with approximately 2,000 tons of sea water from an unlocated leak in the hull. This water had disintegrated the paper bags and caused the chemicals to be released and mixed with the sea water.

The vessel was steaming for Newport News, Virginia for repairs but due to the danger of the pesticide being released into local waters, the ship was denied entry into Chesapeake Bay until the hazard could be eliminated. The *Maria Costa* was held a few miles off shore until the extent of contamination among the crew could be determined. Testing revealed that some crew members who had attempted to pump the contaminated water overboard were affected by the chemicals. The ship had to anchor off shore until the problem could be corrected.

Divers conducted a survey on the hull and found horizontal cracks on the port side. A wooden patch was placed over the cracks to seal the hull and the contaminated water pumped into a barge alongside the ship. After the contaminants were removed they were towed off shore and dumped 250 miles at sea. The *Maria Costa* was brought into port and placed in drydock where repairs to the hull were completed.

Above: On December 15, 1976, the Liberian tanker *Argo Merchant* grounded on the shoals 29 miles southeast of Nantucket Island. The vessel was 18 miles off course. Three days later the winds picked up and waves were washing over the ship. **Below:** On the night of December 20th, rough weather moved into the area and the next morning the tanker split in two spilling seven and one half million gallons of bunker oil into the Atlantic. The ship was never salvaged as the fast moving currents buried the hull on the Nantucket Shoals. *Photos courtesy of the U.S. Coast Guard.*

Above: The oil barge Bouchard-B-No.65, carrying 3.3 million gallons of home heating oil, ran aground off Wings Neck in Buzzards Bay, south of the Cape Cod Canal on the night of January 28, 1977. The cargo tanks were holed and leaking. Another barge was brought alongside to unload the oil from the Bouchard barge. **Below:** The oil spill was in patches and drifted around Buzzards Bay. To avoid further pollution, the Coast Guard attempted to burn the oil with a wicking agent atop the ice. About 2,000 gallons of oil were burned but the pollution in the air seemed to be worse than the oil in the water. *Photos by the Author.*

Above: The coastal tanker *Vincent Tibbetts* went aground on the rocks at Cow Island, just outside Portland, Maine on August 3, 1977. The vessel was carrying 2,900 barrels of oil at the time. She was pulled off the rocks the next day, without damage, by the tug *Celtic*. There was no oil spill in the accident. *Photo courtesy of Guy Gannett Publications, Portland Maine.* **Below:** The last of the sidewheel steamboats from the Hudson River came near to being enshrined as a museum but nature played some bad tricks on her. The steamer *Alexander Hamilton* lay grounded on a sandbar near the shore at Atlantic Highlands, New Jersey for years. In 1977, in an effort to save the historic vessel, she was hauled off the bar and towed to a berth at Earle, New Jersey for temporary berthing. In 1978 a violent storm caught the veteran ship in an exposed position and damaged her beyond repair and she sank. *Photo by the Author.*

Above: The Coast Guard cutter *Cuyahoga* had a long and distinguished career in the service stretching over 51 years. Her service came to an abrupt end on the night of October 20, 1978. Steaming in Chesapeake Bay, the cutter was in a collision with the Argentine coal carrier *Santa Cruz II* and she sank minutes after the accident. Eleven men went down with the cutter. A salvage operation raised the vessel and she was taken to deep water off the Virginia Capes and sunk. A fitting end to a proud ship. **Below:** On February 18, 1979, four airmen aboard a Coast Guard HH-3F helicopter were killed when their aircraft crashed into the Atlantic Ocean. The helicopter was on a rescue mission 180 miles southeast of Cape Cod in thick weather. The sea was rough and, at the time of the accident, the aircraft was hovering over a fishing vessel to remove an injured crewman. A huge wave struck the nose of the aircraft on the right side and it rolled into the sea. One airman from the helicopter survived. *Photos courtesy of the U.S. Coast Guard.*

CHAPTER ELEVEN

WRECKS ON THE BOTTOM

On the bottom of the continental shelf, there are scattered the remains of thousands of shipwrecks. In the three centuries of maritime trade along the Atlantic coastline, countless ships have met their fate here and the rotting bones of the 18th and 19th century square riggers serve as an enticement for 20th century divers who scour the bottom in search of treasure. There is an old adage which states: One man's trash is another man's treasure. Much of what is brought up by amateur divers would not be worth very much to the layman but to a maritime collector, a deadeye or a belaying pin from an early wreck is considered a form of wealth. The value is enhanced if the wreck is identified.

There are hundreds of amateurs who practice their hobby on weekends and probe deep along the ocean's floor. A wide range of professional people is actively engaged in SCUBA diving. Scientists and archaeologists are among these and they dive in hopes of adding to man's knowledge of the bottom of the sea. The amateurs are usually looking for souvenirs for their collections; brass portholes and steering wheels, binnacles, bells and propellers are but a few of the valued finds made on the bottom. The amateur diver usually explores the areas where there have been reports of wrecks. Others hunt for hulls that have never been discovered. The latter are preferred, for the diver has his choice of the relics. After a find, the diver brings it up, cleans it and displays it with the rest of his collection.

Amateur diving is assumed to be a harmless pastime but many archaeologists disagree. A British man-o-war sank during the American revolution in waters off Montauk Point at the tip of Long Island, New York. Amateur divers were reported to have torn apart some rigging and used crowbars to pry loose cannonballs aboard the sunken wreck. Most of the ancient wrecks do not contain any valuable treasure but are important in the study of this country's heritage. Around the entrance to New York harbor there are thousands of historic shipwrecks on the bottom. Most of these are buried under a few feet of sand and silt. Most are well preserved and are considered to be time capsules that preserve early pictures of maritime life on the Atlantic coast.

On the sea floor along the Atlantic coastline there are several W.W,II enemy submarines which were depth charged by the Navy and Coast Guard. Most of them still have their crews aboard. Divers explore inside these silent tombs and bring back photographs taken inside the sunken hulls. The dials and gauges on the control panels often tell a graphic story of conditions aboard when the U-boat sank. Other pictures show the skeletons of the silent crew, mute evidence of the horrors of war. This is a fascinating and dangerous dive but the artifacts brought up are highly valued.

Today's salvagers no longer rely on chance to find shipwrecks at the bottom of the ocean. The use of new scientific instruments is widespread, not only for searching the sea floor but beneath the shifting sands on the bottom. Side scan sonar emits an acoustic beam which is narrow in the horizontal and wide in the vertical planes. This beam is projected out across the sea floor and by receiving reflected echoes, prints a remarkably accurate picture of the sea bed and the objects lying on it. In order to probe down under the ocean floor, the magnetometer is used. It can sense anomalies in the earth's magnetic field as it is affected by ferrous objects that are buried under the surface.

The use of side scan sonar by divers in search for sunken wrecks on the bottom of the Atlantic ocean has turned up finds from Cape Cod to Florida and some of the treasure salvagers have hit it big while others are still looking. An editorial in the New York Times on Aug. 3, 1984 gave an interesting sidelight into the "Sunken Treasures":

"There was a time when movies featuring galleons, Spanish gold, swordplay, storms and a giant octopus were Saturday afternoon staples. They were often based on a novel by Rafael Sabatini, the hero was often Errol Flynn, and if the heroine wasn't Olivia de Havilland it was because it was Paulette Goddard.

"They're brought to mind by two recent underwater happenings.

"First, a salvager reported finding the wreck of the *Whidah*, which sank in a storm off the coast of Massachusetts in 1717. The ship is said to have carried pirate treasure doubloons and assorted jeweled necklaces according to the movie script.

"A few days later another group of salvagers announced they'd found the wreckage of a British warship, the *de Braak*, off the coast of Delaware. A storm did in the *de Braak* too, in 1798, and old accounts say it was packing a fortune in gold, silver and gems.

"Recovering both treasures, assuming they exist at all, will be difficult in the murky waters and thick layers of silt. Hollywood's treasure hunters worried about the giant octopus; their real-life counterparts harbor a more prosaic fear that years of study and searching, not to mention hefty cash investments, will produce no more than a few crusty cannonballs and a mere handful of those tantalizing doubloons."

The discovery of the 18th century British Naval Brig *de Braak* was of major archaeological significance. She sank off Delaware on May 25, 1798 with the loss of thirty-six men. In 1984, a team of divers found the wreck and brought up gold coins, cannons, porcelain, glass and other artifacts. One of the most valuable finds was the engraved gold ring of Captain James Drew. This piece positively identified the wreck. The project required three years of research and months of exploration in the waters off Lewes, Delaware.

One of the most valuable undersea discoveries occurred in 1980, forty miles west of Key West, Florida when Mel Fisher's group found the remains of the treasure from the Spanish galleon *Santa Margarita*. The ship was wrecked in 1622 and the gold recovered was reported to be worth about twenty million dollars. Most of the galleon's silver was salvaged by 17th century divers but the gold eluded them. The company, originally owned by Mel Fisher, is Treasure Salvors, Inc. of Key West and the 1980 discovery was only the beginning. In 1985, Fisher's men found the long lost sister ship to the *Santa Margarita*. A rich hoard of silver bars from the *Nuestra Senora de Atocha* was discovered along with coins and artifacts reported to be worth in excess of 400 million dollars. Considered to be the "Mother Lode" by all treasure hunters the find was not without its cost to Mel Fisher. He had spent over twenty years looking for the ships and had lost his oldest son to drowning in the search.

In the past few years, the new sophisticated underwater surveying instruments have opened up a wide field in the search for sunken treasure ships. The reports of multi-million dollar discoveries on the bottom of the ocean excited the imaginations of a multitude of armchair swashbucklers. Under the gilt however, lies reality. Countless hours of extensive research are necessary in the dusky backrooms of maritime museums to sort out information and establish data about the early voyages. Months and sometimes years are needed to find the remains of vessels lying deep in the ocean.

New expeditions seeking vast underwater wealth were directed by entrepreneurs with get-rich-quick schemes that would lure the rich investor. The unwary sink their money into the new ventures with the only guarantee being a tax write-off. It has been alleged that some groups had salted underwater wrecks with artifacts to enhance the claims of potential treasure. National media headlines of discoveries described the gold mine to be found in the lost Spanish galleons, but the value estimates are seldom backed up by the materials recovered. The fascination of sunken treasure brings out promotions from prestigious brokerage firms, ads in the Wall Street Journal and video cassettes of undersea remains.

Some wreck hunters have actually located ancient shipwrecks. But diving operations are notoriously expensive. Large investments are expended in a few short weeks. After that, the original investors can only take their tax write-off while the entrepreneurs are out looking for new capital to continue their search. Other problems have dogged the treasure salvors. Telephones have been bugged, wreck research stolen and fist fights on the docks between rival salvagers looking for the same wreck. The wreck hunters have filed charges in the courts and the litigation seems to have no end.

Authentic pirate treasure, if it exists, would be a fascinating discovery. There are legends and tall tales of pirate gold on every shoreline along the Atlantic coast. Some of the names of the better known buccaneers imbued terror in the hearts of the sailors of yesteryear; Captain William Kidd, Henry Morgan, Jean Lafitte and the legendary Edward Teach, better known as Blackbeard the pirate. Among the pirate myths is the aura of buried treasure. If they ever did bury it, its likely they came back and recovered it. They kept few if any records or log books for historians to study. The reports passed down by survivors tell most of the stories of the sea robbers. They were the terrorists of their era who answered to no authority higher than their own.

On Cape Cod, off the coast of Wellfleet, Massachusetts, salvagers reported finding the wreckage of the pirate ship *Whidah*. The ship was wrecked on April 17, 1717, in a northeast storm with the loss of all but two of a crew of one-hundred forty-six men. In the summer of 1983, the salvage group began blowing holes in the sea bed off shore, using prop wash deflectors, to find the lost treasure of the *Whidah*. The work continued each summer without any significant finding until October 1985, when divers brought up a bronze bell which had the raised letters: "THE WHYDAH GALLY", around the top. Numerous other artifacts were unearthed from the area, buried in eight feet of sand in Atlantic waters, twenty feet deep. About six thousand silver coins, several cannons, guns and tableware were dug out of the hole in the sea floor. The authentication of the articles was in question as early records indicate that the *Whidah* broke up when she struck the outer bars off Cape Cod and that the wreckage was scattered over a wide area. There are approximately three to four thousand hulls interred along the Cape Cod coastline between Provincetown and Chatham and many of these were strewn helter skelter when wrecked. It has also been documented that the Cape Cod wreckers were at the beach on the morning following the *Whidah* wreck and were working the shoreline. In that era, wrecking was a way of life along the entire Atlantic coast. If the Cape Codders got any of the gold or silver off the *Whidah* they would not have reported it to the authorities. The articles recovered by the Cape Cod salvage group might have come from the pirate ship or could be a collection of relics from a number of vessels that were wrecked in the same area.

The wreck of the *Whidah* on the outer bar on Cape Cod.

The most significant find on the bottom of the Atlantic in recent times is the remains of the steamer *Titanic*, 13,000 feet below the surface, 360 miles off Newfoundland. The 45,000 ton liner was lost on her maiden voyage on the night of April 14, 1912 after striking an iceberg. She sank with the loss of 1,503 persons. There were only 703 survivors. Modern technology has enabled scientists to make three successful expeditions to the sunken luxury liner. The first in September, 1985 ,the second in July 1986 and the third in the summer of 1987. French and American scientists aboard the Woods Hole Oceanographic Institution's research vessel *Knoor* directed the initial project. Using a robot submersible vessel deep in the ocean, they succeeded in bringing back eerie photographs of the ill-fated vessel on the bottom of the Atlantic. The wreckage of the ship was scattered over a wide area but the forward two-thirds of the hull was still in one piece.

The second exploration of the *Titanic* was made from the Woods Hole research vessel *Atlantis II*. Using the deep diving submarine Alvin, Dr. Robert Ballard with a two man crew, made several descents, 13,000 feet to the ocean floor. A robot vehicle was used to explore the wreckage of the ship inside and out. Thousands of still photographs and hours of television pictures were made of the remains on the bottom. The robot, dubbed Jason Junior, was tethered to the submarine Alvin by a 250-foot cable and controlled from inside the sub. The robot with its cameras sailed through the interior of the vessel and made spectacular pictures of the grand staircase, crystal chandeliers and the brass steering wheel on the bridge, shining brightly in the vivid lights of the robot submarine. It was theorized that sediments moved by swift ocean currents kept the brass polished. While the little sub roamed around the underwater tomb of 1,503 souls, no human remains were found but the deterioration of the hull was evident in the photographs. In many areas, falls of rust cascaded down the side of the vessel.

In a press conference preceding the expedition, Dr. Ballard stressed the importance of finding some wood intact on the vessel. The significance was obvious as wood at that depth, if preserved by the tremendous pressure and cold temperatures, would initiate further exploration for more ancient vessels. Photographs from the 1985 expedition indicated the wooden decks on the *Titanic* were whole and intact. However, upon close examination in 1986, it was discovered that the decks were completely eaten away by wood boring organisms.

The robot sub made a complete photographic record of the remains of the *Titanic*. Beginning at the bow which was nearly buried in the bottom sediments, the tiny sub surveyed the forward deck and then looked into the crow's nest where two men had spotted the iceberg on that "Night to Remember". Working aft, the remote controlled cameras recorded pictures of the bridge, near where Captain Edward J. Smith was last seen, going down with his ship. It was discovered that the ship had broken, just aft of the number three smokestack and out beyond there, a huge debris field was littered with thousands of items scattered over the ocean floor. A shoe was seen along with chamber pots, wine bottles, dishes, silver platters, coffee cups, pieces of coal and some of the ship's boilers. The largest piece in the debris field was the 150-foot long stern section which severed from the ship after she sank.

There were other important discoveries. A close examination of the forward part of the hull below the water line failed to find the 300-foot long gash, supposedly caused when the ship collided with the iceberg. The new theory put forth was that the ice fractured the steel plates and they buckled. Rivets popped out and the vessel was opened up to the sea. The general condition of the hull was very fragile as it continued to rust. No paint was found anywhere on the ship. The expedition spent 33 hours on the bottom surveying the *Titanic*, and following this declared that the wreck should not be touched and would be better left as a memorial to the persons who perished when the ship sank.

There are new proposals to raise the *Titanic*. The photographs of the wreck show extensive deterioration of the hull sections. The conditions at the site as outlined by the scientists should preclude any such undertaking. Legislation was introduced in the United States Congress to prevent the wreck being disturbed by poachers. However, enforcement of any U.S. law on the high seas would be questionable. From the few living of the 703 survivors came the impassioned plea: "Leave it alone".

This, however, was not to be. In July, 1987, a team of French salvagers operating from the research ship *Nadir* began a series of dives at the site of the *Titanic* using a small submarine named Nautile. The purpose of the expedition was to retrieve artifacts from the bottom and display them in a museum. Members of the Titanic Historical Society called the operations piracy and grave robbing. The gravesite of the *Titanic* is not protected by international law and it is doubtful that such a law could be enforced even if one were written and enacted. The little submarine descended to the ocean floor and brought up about 300 artifacts consisting of dinnerware, jewelry, a chandelier and other pieces of historic interest. Given today's technology it was inevitable that there would be some recovery of these articles. It is probably better to have a reputable display in a museum than to commercialize the operation and put the artifacts on the open market. There is still a possibility of this happening as further trips to the site are being planned by others. The expeditions cost in the millions of dollars. This would make any artifact brought up and placed on the auction block much too expensive for the average collector.

The passage of time since the loss of the *Titanic* has not dulled the interest in this great ship. She has been the subject of several books, news stories, motion pictures and television programs and continues to make headlines every year. In all histories of notable disasters, the *Titanic* stands out as one of the most important in the maritime field. Much of the data is fact but more is legend, created by the tabloids; the ship was classed as unsinkable. Captain Smith was a hero to many for his actions during the sinking but he had pushed his ship at top speed in spite of repeated warnings of icebergs. The ship's orchestra was playing "Nearer, My God, to Thee" as the vessel foundered, witnesses said it was "Autumn". Chaos ensued on deck during the lowering of the lifeboats, the call was "women and children first", but many of the first class male passengers survived. Scholars have been separating fact from legend for years but the popular beliefs prevail and will probably outlive the historians. The discoveries of the scientists and the intriguing photographs will be studied carefully. Later, more books will be written, but the popular legends of the *Titanic* will probably never be put to rest.

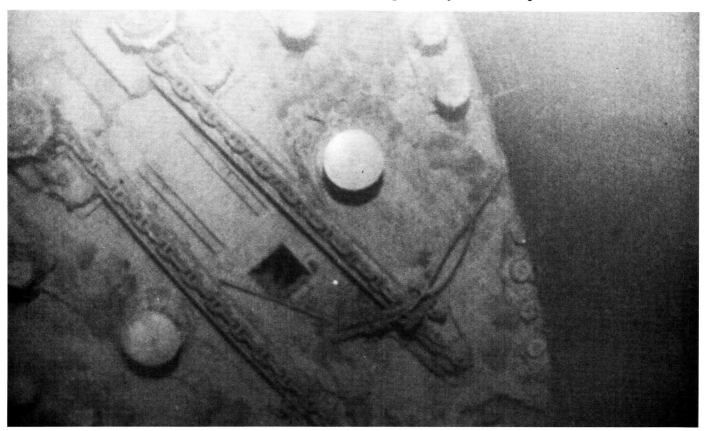

This view was made by the underwater deep-towed camera vehicle ARGO in September, 1985 during the first exploration on the *Titanic*. This is the bow section of the ship and shows the port and starboard bow chains and capstans. *Photo courtesy of the Woods Hole Oceanographic Institution.*

Making pictures underwater that are recognizable by the layman is not an easy task. The photographer has to contend with many different obstacles to registering an image on film. It is obvious that the camera has to go underwater and requires a housing to protect it from the eroding effects of salt water. The diver has to have access to the levers and dials to make proper exposures. The most perplexing problem, however, is light. The deeper the camera goes, the amount of available light for photographs is reduced. Most divers today use a strobe light when making pictures below twenty feet. This equipment is expensive but necessary.

The ideal camera for underwater photography is the 35 millimeter format. The equipment comes in many different makes but the size of the film is constant. The camera is compact and easy to handle. The lens used most is the wide angle which has an extended depth of field. This minimizes the problems of focus in difficult situations. The underwater housing keeps the equipment dry while the diver makes his pictures on the bottom. There are cameras like the Nikonos, built to go underwater without a housing but changing film while on the bottom is not reccommended.

The pictures the diver makes depend primarily on the conditions prevailing on location at the time. The best time to shoot is near the middle of the day in the summertime. The sun is highest and the light penetration the greatest at depths down to two hundred feet. Conditions of observation vary greatly at different locations. Sometimes the diver will encounter unlimited visibility while at other times he may not see more than twelve inches in the same location. The diver has to be careful not to disturb the sediments that settle on the bottom near where he wants to make a photograph as the movement clouds vision and makes a good picture impossible. When the picture is important a good photographer brackets his exposures to be sure he achieves good results. A good rule to remember is that diving time is more expensive than film.

The following sixteen pages are color photographs, most of which were taken underwater by divers Brian Skerry of Uxbridge, Massachusetts and Arnold Carr of Monument Beach, Massachusetts, and are copyrighted. The color photos are concluded with several scenes of the wreck of the *Titanic* which are also copyrighted photographs, courtesy of the Woods Hole Oceanographic Institution. The photographic collection was chosen from a large selection in order to present a clear view of the environment on the bottom of the ocean.

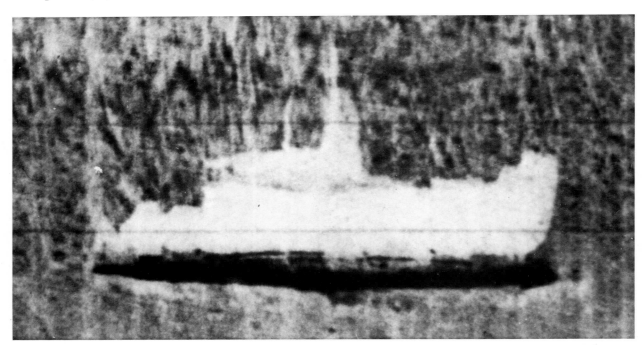

An illustration of side scan sonar. The acoustic beam is narrow in the horizontal and wide in the vertical planes. The beam is projected out across the sea floor and by receiving reflected echoes, prints a picture like the one above of the German submarine U-853, which lies 127 feet deep, seven miles east of Block Island, Rhode Island. The U-boat was sunk by U.S. Naval forces on May 6, 1945. This area is one of the popular spots for divers on the northeast coast. The side scan sonar illustration was made by Gary Kozak. *Photo courtesy of Arnold Carr.*

Above: Swimming down to the underwater world, two divers descend the anchor line of the boat in the background. This is a fish eye view from down underneath the surface of the water. The photograph was taken at a depth of approximately twenty feet. **Below:** At a depth of seventy feet, the former harbor tugboat *Jay Scutti* lies on the bottom off Ft. Lauderdale, Florida. The vessel was sunk intentionally on September 19, 1986 for use as an artificial reef. On the forward deck a diver is inspecting the hull. *Photos by Brian Skerry, Uxbridge, Massachusetts.*

Above: Two divers swimming behind the roof of the pilot house of the *Jay Scutti*. The surfaces of this structure are being coated with marine growths while small fish swim around and through the open windows. **Below:** A barracuda swims lazily through the bridge railing on the *Scutti*. The Florida waters usually provide excellent visibility for photographs. *Photos by Brian Skerry.*

Above: At a depth of 120 feet, two divers enter the crew's space hatch of the *U.S.S. Tarpon* which sank in a storm in August, 1957, while under tow to the scrap yard. **Below:** A view of the diver after entering the hatch with his hands over his head holding tools. This submarine is a favorite spot for divers off the Carolina coast. It is about twenty-two miles from Ocracoke Inlet. *Photos by Brian Skerry.*

Above: Another photograph aboard the *Tarpon* with diver Charlie LeDuc near the stern torpedo loading hatch cover. The hatch is not open. **Below:** A small fish swimming by a broken ladder aboard the wreckage of the Standard Oil Company tanker *F. W. Abrams*. The ship lies off Cape Hatteras at a depth of about 85 feet. This vessel sank after hitting a mine on June 11, 1942. Her crew of 36 was saved. A photograph of the vessel sinking appears on page 125. *Photos by Brian Skerry.*

Above Left: A diver going over the side of the dive boat off the coast of North Carolina with his back full of gear. **Above Right:** This photo was made at a depth of ten feet as several divers are holding on to the anchor line of the dive boat. The men are decompressing after diving deep in the Gulf Stream. **Below:** Diver Bill Palmer at work on the wreck of the steamer *Proteus* which sank on August 19, 1918, 25 miles south of Hatteras Inlet. It is another favorite of wreck divers off North Carolina. Diver Palmer has his main dive tanks with a pony bottle and decompression ascent line along with a crow bar on his back while trying pry something loose from the ship. *Photos by Brian Skerry.*

Above: Aboard the salvage vessel *Mariner,* off the coast of Delaware Joseph Amaral is tending a surface supplied diver 80 feet below. The man under the water is working on the H.M.S. *de Braak* which sank in 1798 with a fortune in gold aboard. On the left is Harvey Harrington who was in charge of the salvage operation. In the background is a work boat/tender which was the survey team's connection with the shore as the *Mariner* was moored permanently over the wreck. **Below:** On the stern of the tender, one of the 14 cannons is raised from the *de Braak.* Supervising the operation is Harvey Harrington. *Photos courtesy of the Historical Maritime Group of New England.*

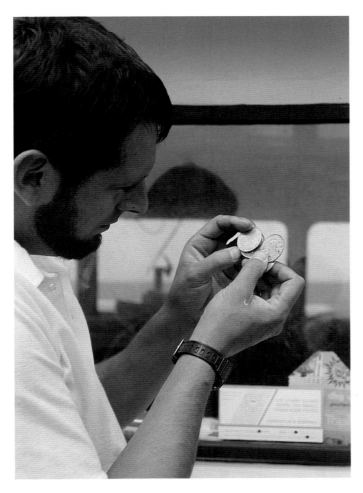

Above Left: Diver, historian John Fish examined some Spanish gold doubloons brought up from the wreck of the *de Braak*. All of the gold coins found were in excellent condition. They were all dated pre 1798. **Above Right:** An arms specialist catalogs parts of guns found on the *de Braak*. The parts were made of brass and provided information on naval equipment of the period. **Below Left:** This plate was identified as "Willow Ware". It was found at a depth of 82 feet at the site of the wreck. The plate is nestled among the debris on the sea floor. **Below Right:** Two views of a man's ring found in the Captain's cabin of the *de Braak*. This artifact helped to positively identify the wreck. The inscription reads:"In memory of a beloved brother, Captain John Drew, drowned 11, Jan. 1798, age, 47." *Photos courtesy of the Historical Maritime Group of New England.*

Above: Near the bow of the schooner barge *Delaware,* Diver Brian Carter poses on the large anchor, fifty feet below the surface. The *Delaware* lies near Collamore Ledge off the coast of Scituate, Massachusetts. She sank during the Portland Gale on November 27, 1898. **Below:** Diver Bill Carter of Marshfield located the whistle of the steamer *Pinthis* on the bottom at a depth of 100 feet. The brass whistle was half buried in the sand but it was a valuable find. *Photos by Brian Skerry.*

Above: The whistle was raised off the bottom using lift-bag lines and brought to the surface. Diver Rusty Carter guided the large brass piece to facilitate handling on the surface. *Photo by Brian Skerry* **Below:** When cleaned up, the whistle presented a different picture. Diver Bill Carter in his den with much of the maritime memorabilia he has acquired through years of sport diving. *Photo by the Author.*

Above: On July 22, 1892, the Vanderbilt yacht *Alva* was sunk in a collision on Pollock Rip Shoals off Chatham, Massachusetts. The hull was destroyed with dynamite because it was a menace to navigation. The spot is a favorite of divers today. Diver Dave Arnold is with photographer Brian Skerry exploring the remains of the hull. Brian is back to with his camera in his left hand. **Below:** Diver, Historian John Fish examines the remains of the bark *Harriet S. Jackson* which sank in September, 1898 off Monomoy Island in Chatham, Massachusetts. *Photos by Arnold Carr.*

Above Left: Before the sand is cleared away, a shipwreck appears to be a line of posts but in reality are the ribs of the hull attached to the keel. **Below:** After the sand is blown away, the shape of the framework of the vessel is recognizable. This is the remains of the British bark *White Squall,* sunk in a storm off Wellfleet Massachusetts in February, 1867. **Above Right:** The cargo of the vessel was reported to be over two thousand ingots of block tin. This piece was found near the stern of the wreck. *Photos by Arnold Carr.*

Above Left: Divers discovered the wheel house of the fishing vessel *Katherine Marie,* about seventy feet down on the bottom of Cape Cod Bay, four miles northeast of the Cape Cod Canal. **Below:** Inside the cabin the working gear seems to be intact with a thin film of marine growth beginning to appear on the surfaces of the gear. **Above Right:** One of the most easily recognizable artifacts of marine memorabilia is the ship's wheel. Divers found this among the wreckage of the schooner *Sagamore* which went down off Martha's Vineyard following a collision with the Norwegian steamer *Edda* on May 10, 1907. *Photos by Arnold Carr.*

Above-Left: On April 14, 1985, at the Fall River Marine Museum, a ceremony was held celebrating the unveiling of a 28-foot long model of the *Titanic*, which was used in the 1953 Hollywood motion picture. **Above-Right:** Attending the event was Mrs Majorie N. Robb, of Westport, Massachusetts, a survivor of the sinking of the *Titanic*. Mrs Robb was a child at the time and she lost her father when the ship went down. She autographed books about the *Titanic* for the visitors at the museum that night but declined to pose with the model of the ship. **Below:** In July, 1986, Dr. Robert Ballard of the Woods Hole Oceanographic Institution met with the press aboard the research vessel *Atlantis II*, to explain the underwater craft being used in the search for the *Titanic*. He stood in front of the submarine *Alvin*. Under his elbow is the remote controlled submarine Jason junior. This was prior to the second expedition to the *Titanic*. *Photographs by the Author.*

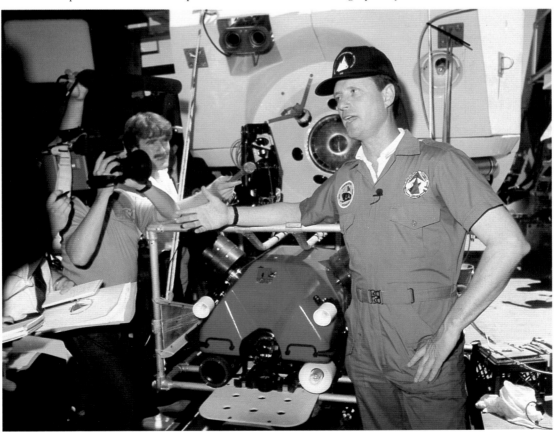

Above: Out in the Atlantic, 350 miles south of Newfoundland, the submarine *Alvin,* at sea, after being launched from the *Atlantis II* which is in the background. There are two swimmers in wet suits tending the submarine, prior to the dive. A photographic essay was presented in the December 1986 issue of the National Geographic Magazine using several color pictures from this expedition. **Below Left:** Near the bow of the ship, the submarine *Alvin* photographed the anchor of the *Titanic* hanging on the starboard side. Small tentacles of rust make the flukes appear to have weeds growing around them. **Below Right:** The erosion of the hull of the *Titanic* at the depth of thirteen thousand feet has continued for the seventy-five years she has been on the bottom. Dr. Robert Ballard referred to the phenomenon as "rivers of rust". This rust hangs like stalactites as it spills down in front of the portholes. The Oceanographic Institution called the deterioration "rust sickles." This rust, however, could be an attempt by nature to symbolically cover-up the disaster which took so many lives. The pictures taken on the bottom are alien to the untrained eye and probably look bizarre or supernatural. *Photos courtesy of the Woods Hole Oceanographic Institution.*

Above: A view from the submarine *Alvin* of the remote controlled Jason Jr. as the tiny craft left the mother ship to descend into the interior of the *Titanic.* The yellow cable is a tether used to control the movements of the small submersible. **Below:** With *Alvin* resting on the boat deck of the *Titanic,* Jason Jr. made a spectacular photograph of the side of the ship at what appears to be a strange looking growth but, in reality, is more rust cascading down the side of the ship. *Photographs courtesy of the Woods Hole Oceanographic Institution.*

Above: Underwater cameras photographed two bollards and part of the railing on the starboard side of the *Titanic* near the bow. The "rivers of rust" cover almost all of the surfaces of the ship on the bottom. **Below Left:** A copper kettle from the galley of the *Titanic* lay in the debris field a third of a mile south off the bow of the liner. Strong bottom currents and particles in the water kept the kettle polished so that it appears almost new. This kettle was later shown on world wide television, on October 28, 1987, being salvaged by the French expedition. **Below Right:** One of the most spectacular pictures taken aboard the *Titanic* was made by the remote control vehicle Jason Jr. After descending the grand staircase into the interior of the ship, the camera recorded this growth encrusted chandelier, still hanging by a thin wire. This photograph was later shown to the world on television news broadcasts. *Photographs courtesy of the Woods Hole Oceanographic Institution.*

 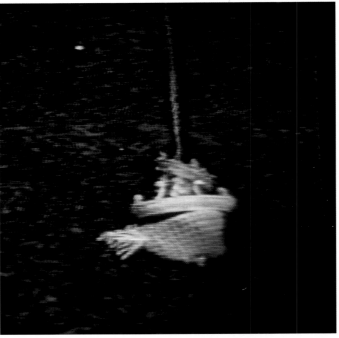

CHAPTER TWELVE

Another Atlantic storm churned up the ocean off the Virginia coast on February 12, 1983. The bulk carrier *Marine Electric* was carrying 24,800 tons of coal from Norfolk, Virginia to Somerset, Massachusetts when it ran into the storm and began to take on water. The ship was a 39-year old converted tanker and was not considered to be overloaded. The vessel was hove-to in 40 m.p.h. winds and 15-18 foot seas about thirty miles off Chincoteague. The conditions grew worse and the ship was low in the bow. Shortly after 4 a.m., the crew were forced to abandon ship. When they attempted to launch a lifeboat, the ship rolled over and the entire crew were thrown into the sea. Coast Guard helicopters from Elizabeth City, North Carolina were dispatched to the scene. When the helicopters arrived they found one lifeboat empty and a second one with one man aboard. Three rafts were spotted and there were many crewmen in the water with lifejackets on. The death toll was high. Thirty-one of the crew had perished and only three survived. They were identified as Eugene S. Kelly, 31, of Norwell, Mass.; Paul C. Dewey, 28, of Grandby, Conn.; and Robert M. Cusick, 59, of Scituate, Mass. All three were suffering from hypothermia, a severe loss of body temperature. The *Marine Electric* was owned by the Marine Coal Transport Company of Wilmington, Delaware. During the subsequent investigation by the Coast Guard it was revealed that the hatch covers were warped and riddled with holes. The ship was taking heavy seas over her bow before she capsized and sank in the Atlantic.

As a result of the *Titanic* tragedy in 1912, the United States Coast Guard began the ice patrol on the steamship lanes in the north Atlantic in 1913. The patrol continues to this day. The cutters have been replaced by aircraft with modern radar which can locate icebergs, even in dense fog. The area covered by the patrol is about 45,000 square miles. An average of 400 icebergs drift into the steamer routes each year between February and August. The bergs are all plotted on a chart with the position and drift. One inherent danger is the growlers, or icebergs with little mass above water. These are invisible to radar and thus difficult to plot.

Icebergs are still a menace over which man has no control. They break off from the huge glaciers of Greenland and float along, moved by ocean currents. Some are as big as a city block. They cannot be destroyed or held back. Different solutions have been sought for the iceberg problem. The Coast Guard tried bombing them in an attempt to break them into smaller pieces. The theory was that they would ultimately melt faster but the bombs exploded harmlessly. Many other experiments were tried but the icebergs kept coming. The only solution was to let nature take its course and maintain the present patrols and plotting to warn the ships at sea.

Recent technology has improved safety at sea but electronics play a major role in maritime operations today. The gyrocompass took much of the guesswork out of navigation and enabled ships to steer a true course. Sonar was used in World War I to detect submarines but was erratic, and not dependable, until scientists discovered the thermoclines. In World War II, sonar was then an asset. Further advances in sonar enable fishing vessels to find schools of fish underwater. Radar is a beam of electronic impulses which bounce off metal targets and these appear as blips on a receiver screen. There are many types of radar in use and most ships are equipped with a navigational type today. Weather radar plots storms for improved forecasting. Loran, or long range navigation, is an electronic system which determines location at sea. By using loran charts, the data is electronically computed to establish a ship's position. The space age has brought satellite navigation. The satellites orbit 600 miles above the earth and continuously broadcast their positions. The computers aboard ship give the latitude and longitude. This system has relegated the traditional instruments of celestial navigation to the dark ages. A navigator is no longer really needed aboard ship except as a backup to the electronics.

Above: On May 9, 1980, at 7:34 a.m., the 20,000 ton freighter *Summit Venture* destroyed a portion of the Sunshine Skyway bridge across Tampa Bay in Florida, killing 35 people. The 608 foot long ship was heading up the bay in a blinding rainstorm when she struck the bridge. Seven automobiles and a Greyhound bus along with 1,200 feet of roadway toppled into the bay. **Below:** The *Summit Venture* after the accident with part of the roadway and bridge girders draped over her bow. The anchor was dropped previous to the accident in an effort to stop the ship before it ran into the bridge. *Official U.S. Coast Guard Photos by AE3 M.W. Spetz.*

The Panamanian freighter *Ocean Endeavour* lost power during a coastal storm and ran aground on Island Beach, New Jersey on October 25, 1980. There were no injuries to any of her crewmen in the grounding. There were, however, problems inland from the storm. Massive power outages along the coastline and extra high tides forced the evacuation of thousands along the Atlantic coastline. The freighter was pulled off the beach two days later and returned to service. *Photo by John de Santo, Asbury Park Press.*

The maritime heritage of the United States began in the seventeenth century in colonial America. Communication in the thirteen colonies was mostly by sea and rivers. The marine commerce opened up trade routes along the Atlantic coast and the people prospered. Fishing, whaling and shipbuilding grew into big business. Seaports sprung up near settlements as more and more people emigrated to the new world and America became a "melting pot" of millions of people. The country progressed into independence and advanced to a world power through hard work and technology. Our maritime heritage today consists of literature, carvings, scrimshaw, seamanship, music, ship models and paintings. This treasure is preserved and maintained in the various marine museums along our country's coastlines. They support research programs and conduct symposiums in the search for maritime history. They house a wealth of historic memorabilia.

In addition to Marine Museums, there are many historic ships which have been restored and are open to visitors who wish to go aboard and see part of our maritime heritage. In some cases, replicas have been made of older vessels. In Boston, Massachusetts there are two vessels which welcome tourists. Perhaps the most famous is the *U.S.S. Constitution,* better known as "Old Ironsides." She is the oldest ship in commission in the United States Navy. She was launched on September 20, 1797 and she fought in the war of 1812. The vessel mounts 44 guns and is 175 feet long. The other historic vessel in Boston is the replica of the Boston Tea-Party brig *Beaver.* The original vessel served as a base of the famous Indian raid to protest the tea tax levied by Britain in 1773. This and other events led to the revolution and independence for the United States of America. Moving south from Boston, at Plymouth lies the full scale replica of the Pilgrim ship called *Mayflower II.* One can go aboard and see what life was like back in 1620 when the 102 passengers crowded aboard the tiny ship and came across the Atlantic. Southwest from Plymouth at Fall River, the Battleship *Massachusetts* lies in Battleship Cove along with a destroyer and a submarine.

A short drive from Fall River to the west lies Mystic Seaport in Connecticut. Two magnificent square rigged sailing ships are on display. An early shipbuilding and whaling port, Mystic Seaport today is one of the largest maritime museums on the Atlantic coast. The only surviving nineteenth century wooden whaling ship afloat is the *Charles W. Morgan*. This vessel along with the full rigged ship *Joseph Conrad* are the central attractions of the flotilla at Mystic Seaport. In New York City at the South Street Seaport Museum there are several large and small ships on display. Two large 19th century square riggers highlight the exhibits. The *Wavertree* and the *Peking* are featured along with lightships, tugboats and ferries with exhibits on modern port activities.

In Philadelphia, Pennsylvania, Admiral Dewey's flagship, the *Olympia* is berthed on the Delaware River near Independence Hall. The *Olympia* is a national shrine and Naval Museum. Nearby is the square rigged barkentine *Gazela Primeiro*, the last of her type from the Portuguese fishing fleet. The *Gazela Primeiro* is owned by the Philadelphia Maritime Museum. At Baltimore, the *Constellation*, sister ship to the *Constitution* lies at the dock on Pratt Street and is open to the public year round. The Smithsonian Institution in Washington, D.C. houses an interesting artifact at the National Museum of History and Technology on 14th street. The Continental gunboat *Philadelphia* was built in 1776 and was sunk in Lake Champlain during the battle of Valcour Island. The vessel was recovered from the lake in relatively good condition and is on display as she was raised. Further south the coastline juts out along the outer banks and the Cape Hatteras National Seashore, scene of thousands of shipwrecks over its three hundred plus year history. Located south of Whalebone Junction is Coquina Beach where the remains of the four masted schooner *Laura A. Barnes* lie. Her crew was rescued by the Coast Guard but the ship was a total loss. Much of the keel and bottom planking is preserved. At Wilmington, North Carolina, the battleship BB 55, the *U.S.S. North Carolina* lies at her berth on the Cape Fear River. Visitors can roam through the huge ship and see her engine rooms, the main decks, guns and an evening program of films of the memorable veteran of World War II.

Another memorable World War II vessel is berthed at Patriots Point on Charleston Harbor in South Carolina. The *U.S.S. Yorktown* was known as the "Fighting Lady" and is part of a Naval and Maritime Museum display. A replica of the *H.M.S. Bounty* is berthed at the Vinoy Basin next to the Municipal Pier on Second Avenue in St. Petersburg, Florida. The ship was built for use in the film "Mutiny on the Bounty" and memorabilia from the film are on display on the pier alongside the ship.

The *U.S.S. Olympia* Commodore Dewey's flagship at the Battle of Manila Bay during the Spanish-American War. Located at Penn's Landing, Philadelphia, Pennsylvania. The ship is open to the public.

One of the most prolific areas for shipwrecks is the backside beach of Cape Cod, Massachusetts. On March 29, 1984, the Maltese freighter *Eldia* came ashore in a storm at Nauset Beach in Orleans. The danger of oil spill was quickly dispelled by the Atlantic Strike Force team of the Coast Guard. An H-3 from the air station on Cape Cod assisted the men by carrying equipment to and from the wreck. The vessel was refloated on May 17th. *Photo by the Author.*

Above: The *Morton S. Bouchard, Jr.* sank in the west end of the Cape Cod Canal near the Bourne Bridge on April 11, 1983. The 100-foot tug capsized when it became tangled in the tow cable running to a barge it was towing. The accident happened at night and the seven man crew were all rescued by the two men on the barge. A heavy oil slick spread out throughout the canal and efforts were made to control the spill. **Below:** The barge Century raised the tug off the bottom of the canal a week later and it was towed to a shipyard for repairs. *Photos by the Author.*

Above: An old adage relates that accidents come in three's. Such was the case with sunken tugboats. On July 7, 1983, the tug *Helen McAllister* was run down by her tow in Casco Bay near Portland, Maine. One man was killed when he was trapped in the tug's wheelhouse but the other five crewmen survived the sinking. One week later, the barge Century, which was used to raise the tug in the Cape Cod Canal was in Maine and raised the *McAllister. Photo by Doug Jones, Portland Press Herald.* **Below:** The third tugboat sinking occurred a month later on August 9, 1983. The *Morania 16* sank suddenly while escorting a tanker through the Kill Van Kull, New York. The six man crew was rescued by another tug nearby. Again, a few days later the barge Century, raised the sunken tugboat. The Century is a unique machine designed for salvage work with a large one-hundred ton crane. *Photo courtesy of the U.S. Coast Guard.*

Above: The Honduran freighter *Civonney*, on fire, 270 miles east of Delaware Bay on March 16, 1983. The vessel was spotted by Coast Guard patrol aircraft and intercepted by the cutter *Duane*. Denied permission to board, they stood by until the next morning when the crew of the cutter saw smoke coming from the hold. The freighter's crew abandoned ship in their lifeboat and crewmen from the cutter boarded and tried to save the vessel. **Below:** The *Duane* crewmen extinguished a fire in the engine room of the ship but other fires in the hold and flooding throughout the vessel caused her to sink. The Coast Guard men had to abandon her. After she sank, 52 bales of marijuana came to the surface. This was recovered by the *Duane*. The twenty-one crewmen of the *Civonney* were transported to the mainland and were turned over to Federal Authorities in New Jersey. *Photos courtesy of the U.S. Coast Guard.*

Above: On November 22, 1984 the 190-foot Venezuelan freighter *Mercedes I* ran aground in a posh section of Palm Beach, Florida, during a storm. The ship crashed into a sea wall of the home of Molly Wilmot, next door to the Kennedy family compound. The rusting hulk was as out of place in Palm Beach as a hobo at a society party. The freighter lay on the beach for over three months until salvagers could haul her off. On March 6, 1985 the ship was moved off shore and on March 30th was sunk off Fort Lauderdale to become the 26th artificial reef in the area, created to help fish spawn. **Below:** A 75-foot New Bedford fishing vessel sank at State Pier on December 26, 1984 after it had struck a barge outside the harbor and returned to the pier. Salvagers, using a crane and divers raised the *Capt. Lavoeiro* three days later and pumped her out. *Photos by the Author.*

225

Above: The fishing vessel *Maureen S.* ran aground about three a.m. on the morning of January 20, 1985 near Gay Head beach on Marthas Vineyard, Massachusetts. The Coast Guard removed the five man crew by helicopter and landed them at Falmouth. The vessel was pulled off three days later by a tug. **Below:** The barge Richard K. with 840,000 gallons of gasoline, was adrift off the Rhode Island coast on January 20, 1985 after a cable broke from her tug. A Coast Guard helicopter hovered over the barge, four and a half miles northwest of Block Island, Rhode Island until it was re-attached by towline to her tug and towed to Providence, R.I. *Photos courtesy of the U.S. Coast Guard, Boston, Mass.*

Three helicopters from Air Station Cape Cod participated in a spectacular rescue 210 miles out into the Atlantic when a Soviet freighter, the *Komsomolets Kirgizii* sent out a distress call. The vessel had drifted into the trough of the waves after the engines stopped and the cargo shifted. The first helicopter rescued 15 persons from the stricken ship. The second chopper lifted 16 and the final aircraft picked up the remaining 6 including the Captain. The next day, the ship was not seen by an aerial patrol and was presumed lost. *Photo courtesy of the U.S. Coast Guard.*

Over the past one hundred years, maritime traffic has undergone many changes along the Atlantic coastline but storms continue to take their toll in shipwrecks. The sailing ships have passed into history and the world is a little poorer for their loss. But man is slowly exhausting his energy sources and sail may return in future generations albeit not of the same dimension as in the past. The next vessel driven by the winds may be run by a computer. When compared to the old days, the new sailor will probably never see the end of a yardarm or hear the call for "all hands on deck."

Today's technology has altered traditional shipboard operations at sea. Satellite navigation has all but eliminated the navigator's berth. The lifeboats and breeches buoys have been retired to the museums. Currently the men of the Coast Guard use helicopters and fast cutters to rescue mariners in peril. Perhaps one of the last frontiers for man to conquer lies at the bottom of the ocean. When he solves the mysteries of the depths and can readily explore the sea floor, the remnants of hundreds of years of sea faring will be there to discover. Modern space-age weather forecasting warns the sailor of approaching storms days before they arrive. The latest developments in shipbuilding have further reduced the dangers of shipwrecks. But, as the passengers of the *Titanic* found out too late, no ship is unsinkable.

ACKNOWLEDGMENTS

The collection of photographs in this book was completed over a period of about fifteen years. Many were copied from originals loaned by several friends and several more were purchased. I have traded a few pictures here and there. A few were found in antique auctions and one turned up at a flea market in Maine. There are several friends I wish to extend appreciation to for helping me on this endeavor. They are: Ardie Kelly, Librarian at the Mariners Museum in Virginia; Arnold Carr, John Fish, Brian Skerry, Bill Carter, Elizabeth Peterson, Steven Lang, Capt. W.J.L. Parker, U.S.C.G. (Ret.), Bob Beattie, Brewster Harding, Laura Brown, Richard M. Boonisar, Richard Griggs, Lance Jones, Charlie Sayle, Dick Kelsey, Harry Trask, Mrs. Donald D. Sams, Connie Driscoll, Bill Ewen, Nathan Lipfert, Gordon Caldwell, Capt. Biff Bowker, U.S.C.G. Historian Bob Scheina, Pilot Chuck Scott, John Ullman, Bebe Midget, Bill Peterson and my artist-historian friend Paul C. Morris. I wish to thank the Mariners Museum in Newport News, Virginia, the Maine Maritime Museum in Bath, Maine, the Peabody Museum of Salem and the Fall River Marine Museum of Fall River, Massachusetts and the Steamship Historical Society of America with library in Baltimore, Maryland. These institutions provided me with access to their photo banks to help complete my collection for this volume. Many kind thanks to all.

W.P.Q.

The 94-foot fishing vessel *Kathleen & Julie II* ran up on the rocks of Staples Point in Cape Elizabeth, Maine, at 3:40 a.m. on the morning of September 25, 1984. This vessel was lucky in that she was empty after having unloaded her cargo in Gloucester, Massachusetts. She was floated off at 8:10 a.m. without damage and was taken to the Portland Fish Pier. *Photo by Elizabeth Peterson, Cape Elizabeth, Maine.*

LIST OF PHOTOGRAPHS

A. Ernest Mills 95
Ada Tower ii
Adelaide Day 89
African Queen 167
Alexander Hamilton 193
Alice E. Clark 48
Alice Murphy 18
Alpha 52
Altoona 9
Alva wreck 210
Ambassador 186
America, Liner 83
Amerique 7
Amphialos 175
Ana Maria 167
Andrea Doria 158,159,160
Anna R. Heidritter 119
Antioch 61
Antonin Dvorak 169
Argo Merchant 191
Arizona 11
Atlantic 7
Atlantis 214
Atlantus 87
Australia 121

Bainbridge 91
Belfast 68
Belleville 166
Belogorsk 185
Benjamin F. Poole 15
Beth iv
Black Gull 149
Blanche C. Pendleton 71
Bremen 36
Bristol 14
Byron D. Benson 124

C.G.C. Morrill 84
Canadian Planter 103
Capt. Lavoeiro 225
Carl Gerhard 95
Carroll A. Deering 72
Cayuga 111
Chapultepec 126
Charles A. Dean 88
Charles S. Haight 135
Charles A. Ritcey 70
Cherokee 156
Cibao 90
City of Keansburg 163
City of Rockland 96
City of Salisbury 105
City of Taunton 38
City of Worcester viii
Civonney 224
Clan Galbraith 65
Columbia 26
Commonwealth 58
County of Edinborough 32
Cox and Green 13

Dagmar Salen 138
Daniel Willard 64
Daylight viii
Delaware 208
Diamond Shoals Lightship 30
District of Columbia 141,178
Dixie Arrow 121
Dorothy B. Barrett 67

Edgar S. Foster 27
Eileen Ross 99
Eldia 221
Elias 185
Elna II 163
Empire Knight 132
Empire Thrush 124
Empress Bay 169
Endeavor 149
Essex 116
Esso Brussels 184
Esther Adelaide 79
Etrusco 155

F.W. Abrams 125, 204
F.J. Luckenbach 128
Falcon 112
Falmouth 30
Florida 46
Fort Fetterman 152,153
Fort Mercer 146
Fortuna 50
Frances 4
Frederick R. Kellogg 67

G.A. Kohler vi
Gate City 31
Gem 173
General Slocum 41
George Farwell 43
Gertrude Abbott 12
Golden Gate 40
Governor Carr 108
Governor Herrick 104
Graham 164,165
Gratitude 79
Grigory Lysenko 176

H.C. Higginson 12
Helen McAllister 223
Helga Bolten 161
Henry B. Hyde 40
Henry F. Sinclair 123
Horatio L. Baker 20
Hudson 32

Invermay 63
Irma 82
Iroquois 103

J. Henry Edmunds 50
J. Putnam Bradlee 24
James Duffield 55

James Judge 41
James Longstreet 133
James M.W. Hall 75
James T. Maxwell, Jr. 16
Jason 21
Jay Scutti 201
John F. Kranz 39
John Gibbon 134
Joseph V. Connolly 140

Katie D. 173
Kiowa 39
Komsomolets Kirgizii 227

Lady Barbara 188
Leicester 140
Lester A. Lewis 15
Lewis King 10
Lightburne 109
Lillian 110
Lochinvar 98
Louis Bossert 44

Main 36
Malamton 104
Malden 73
Mandalay 105
Manhattan, liner 114
Marguerite 64
Marine Merchant 172
Marine Sulphur Queen 174
Marion 45
Marjory Brown 62
Mary E. Olys 71
Mary F. Kelly 20
Maryland, tug 182
Mitilda Buck iii
Mattie E. Eaton 13
Maureen & Michael 176
Marueen S., f/v 226
Mayari 76
Melbourn P. Smith 18
Mercedes 225
Metapan 63
Miget 148
Minas Prince 99
Modig 83
Moldegaard 52
Monhegan 107
Morina 16 223
Morro Castle 100,101
Morton S. Bouchard Jr. 222
Musashino Maru 188

Naiad 58
Nantucket 60
Nathaniel T. Palmer 33
New Hampshire 58
Newark 58
Nomis 102
Nora V. 151
Normandie 118,119
Nyland 156

Oakey L. Alexander 136
Ocean Eagle 177
Ocean Endeavour 219
Omar Babun 150
Oregon 117
Oriental-transport 2
Oriental f/v 178

Paraguay 95
Paraporti 157
Paulding 92
Pendleton 147
Penn 61
Pennsylvania Sun 126
Perseus 60
Phoenix, tanker 107
Pilgrim Belle 154
Pine Ridge 171
Plymouth 38
Polias 86
Popi 157
Portland 26
President Hayes 98
Princeton 58
Prinzess Irene 51
Priscilla 28,29
Proteus 205
Purnell T. White 99
Pythian 45

Republic 46
Republica de Columbia 183
Rex 66
Richelieu 88
Rio Branco 111
Ruby 42
Ruth E. Merrill 77

Santa Rosa 168
Santore 125
Sea Witch 184
Shannon 154
Side Scan Sonar Photo 200
Sierra Miranda 78
Sierra Morena 82
Sindia 34
Snetind 110
Sommers N. Smith 22,23
Spartan Lady 187
Squalus 113
St. Paul 66
Stolt Dagali 175
Student Prince 151
Submarine S-19 81
Submarine S-4 92
Submarine S-48 74
Summit Venture 218
Sumner 65
Sylvester F. Whalen 189

Theafano Livanos 145
Thistleroy 53

Thordis Presthus 183	*W.F. Marshall* 8
Tiger 122	*W.N. Reinhardt* 85
Titanic 54,215	*Waldo L. Stream* 80
Transhawaii 183	*Wandby* 73
Trebia 53	*Wanderer* 78
	West Hika 94
U.S.C.G.C.*Cuyahoga* 194	*White Squall* wreck 211
U.S.C.G. Helicopter H-3 194	*Willboro* 102
U.S.N. DE-143 129	*William Bisbee* 89
U.S.N. DE-51 129	*Wyvisbrook* 56
U.S.S.*Greer* 127	
U.S.S.*Grouse* 174	*Yankee* 48
U.S.S.*Missouri* 142	
U.S.S.*Tarpon* 203	*Zulia* 62
Valchem 168	
Vincent Tibbetts 193	
Vincenzo Bonanno 42	

The three year old fishing vessel *Lois Joyce* went aground in Oregon Inlet on the outer banks of North Carolina on December 12, 1982. Captain Walter Tate was fighting 35-50 knot winds with gusts to 70. The seas on the bar were over eight feet. A Coast Guard helicopter from Elizabeth City, N.C. rescued Captain Tate and his five crewmen. The trawler capsized and was a total loss. The photo above was taken in May of 1986 of the remains of the *Lois Joyce*. Loss was estimated at over one million dollars. *Photo by the Author, Plane piloted by Chuck Scott.*